EARLY BUS SERVICES IN ULSTER

Early Bus Services in Ulster

M L KENNEDY

D B McNEILL

THE INSTITUTE OF IRISH STUDIES
THE QUEEN'S UNIVERSITY OF BELFAST
IN ASSOCIATION WITH
THE ULSTER FOLK AND TRANSPORT MUSEUM
1997

Published 1997
The Institute of Irish Studies
The Queen's University of Belfast
in association with the Ulster Folk and Transport Museum

ISBN 0 85389 697 X

Cover design and typesetting
by W & G Baird Ltd, Antrim

Printed by W & G Baird Ltd, Antrim

Early Bus Services in Ulster

CONTENTS **page**

Principal Bus Services in Ulster (1933)

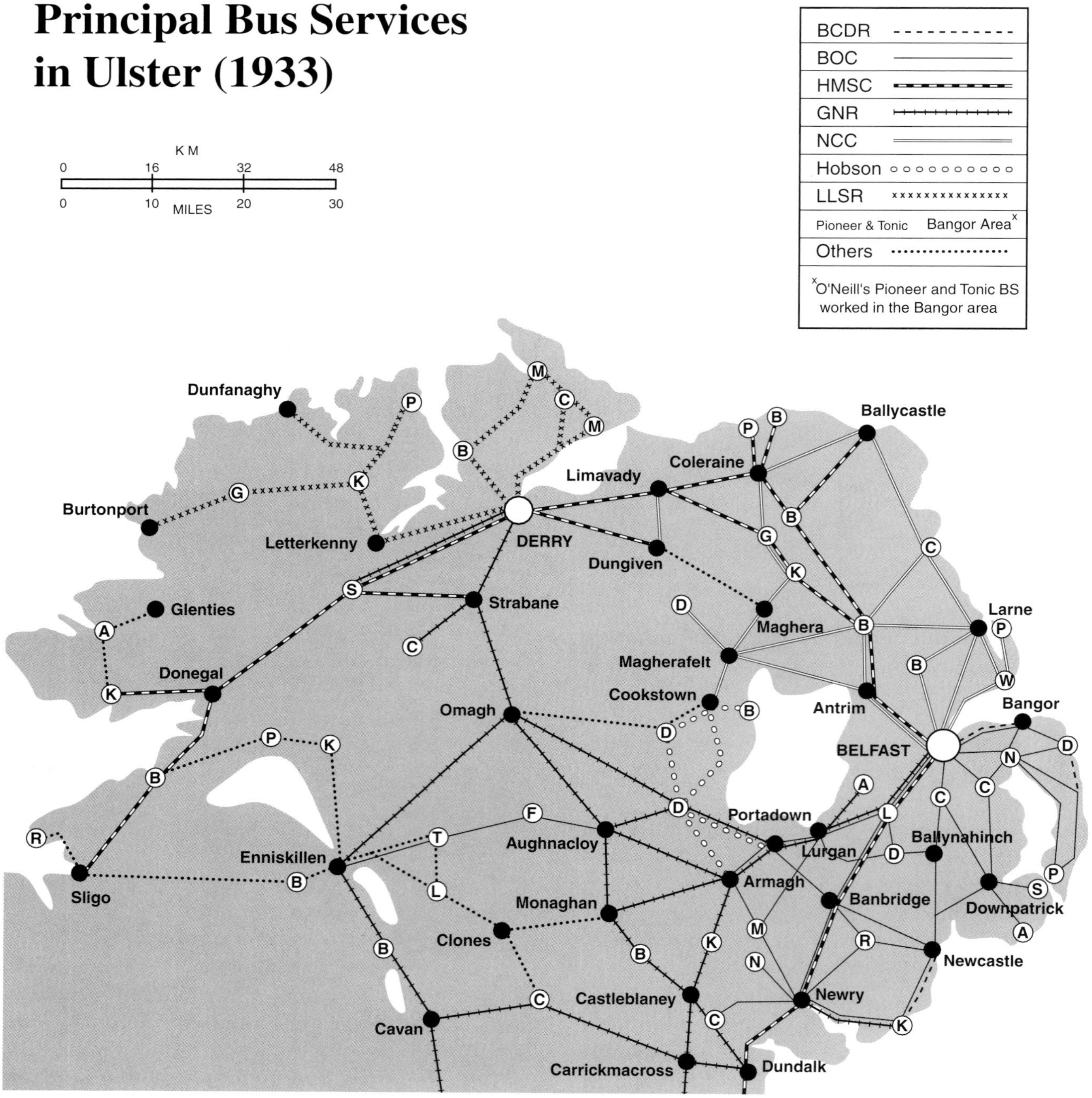

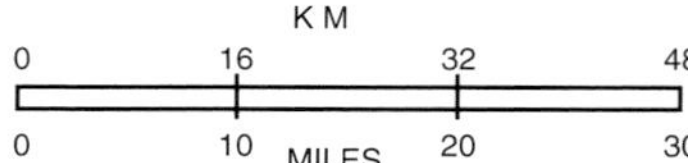

BCDR	- - - - - - - - - -
BOC	———————
HMSC	(heavy dashed line)
GNR	+++++++++++++
NCC	(double line)
Hobson	o o o o o o o o o o
LLSR	xxxxxxxxxxxxxxx
Pioneer & Tonic	Bangor Area[x]
Others	···················

[x]O'Neill's Pioneer and Tonic BS worked in the Bangor area

Dunfanaghy
Burtonport
Letterkenny
DERRY
Limavady
Coleraine
Ballycastle
Dungiven
Glenties
Strabane
Maghera
Larne
Donegal
Magherafelt
Cookstown
Antrim
Omagh
Bangor
BELFAST
Portadown
Aughnacloy
Lurgan
Ballynahinch
Enniskillen
Armagh
Sligo
Banbridge
Downpatrick
Monaghan
Clones
Newcastle
Castleblaney
Newry
Cavan
Carrickmacross
Dundalk

Introduction

1. BNCR horse-drawn omnibus which worked the 2 mile route between Eglinton village and the railway station. It was driven by members of the Harvey family for three generations and mainly used for the conveyance of children to schools and colleges in Derry. (From a postcard). UFTM L579/9

During the twentieth century motor transport has changed from novelty to necessity so that today nearly everyone in Ireland uses it, if not daily, at least once a week. Motor vehicles began to arrive in Ulster in the late 1890s and by 1914 there were regular bus services in the Inishowen and Ards Peninsulas, and many seaside resorts had at least one motor charabanc running tours during holiday periods. The development of civilian motor transport was restricted during the 1914–18 War but, by 1924, motor buses and charabancs had begun to flood into the province during an age when public transport was subject to few regulations other than a 12 mph speed limit. In 1926 some of the principal omnibus proprietors became convinced that the rationalisation of their industry was necessary, and began to take steps which led to the formation of the Belfast Omnibus Company (BOC) in the spring of the next year. A few months before this the Northern Ireland Government had passed the Motor Vehicles (Traffic and Regulations) N.I. Act of 1926 which, beside other provisions, transferred the authority to license public transport from local to central government, therefore permitting anyone operating a bus service anywhere in the province to compete with the Belfast Corporation trams within the city boundary. About 20 omnibus proprietors took advantage of this permission and, between June and December 1928, over 100 buses were jostling with one another, and with the trams, for passengers throughout the city. Finally, all parties concerned came to a mutual understanding that Belfast Corporation would be responsible for the provision of public transport within its city and that, elsewhere

2. One of three Stirling motor buses supplied in 1903 to the Earl of Leitrim to transport guests between his hotel at Rosapenna and Strabane railway station. Ulster Museum, R Welch Collection. WO4/69/16

throughout Northern Ireland, the Stormont government would restrict the issue of licences to services which had been in operation on 27 August 1928. Accordingly, on Monday, 17 December 1928 the Belfast Bus War ended.

Between 1927 and 1935 many of the smaller companies sold their businesses to larger bus operators, eg the BOC, so that the total number of bus owners was reduced from about 180 at the end of 1927 to 72 on 27 February 1935, of whom about a half owned three or more buses, and only eleven owned more than ten vehicles, the largest being the BOC with 148 buses. As this reduction was taking place, the Northern Ireland Government decided to follow the recommendations of Felix Pole's report, *Transport Conditions in Northern Ireland* (Belfast, 1934) to bring all public service road transport, whether passenger or freight, under one ownership. On 16 July 1935 it passed the Road and Railway Transport (NI) Act which set up the Northern Ireland Road Transport Board. In October of that year it began to take over all the bus companies operating in Northern Ireland, the principal exemptions being the transport services owned by Belfast Corporation and companies operating trans-border routes into the Irish Free State. By January 1936 the board had acquired about 700 buses, the owners of which were compensated either in cash or in NIRTB stocks. The amounts paid to each proprietor were published in the board's accounts (see Appendix B) which show that many proprietors had to wait for several years before their accounts were settled. Furthermore, in some instances, it is difficult to deduce on what criteria the final values were based, for even when allowances are made for items such as the goodwill, market value of garages, waiting rooms and offices, there are still wide discrepancies in the value of the compensation paid to individual operators.

3. Ards Motor Transport Co Ltd bus at the Esplanade, Bridge Street, Bangor. Date, c1916. Photographer W A Green. UFTM WAG 3103

The province of Ulster is the most northerly of the four provinces of Ireland. It extends from Malin Head in Donegal to Lough Ramor in County Cavan, a north-south distance of about 100 miles whilst 130 miles separates Malinmore Head, also in Donegal, from Ballyhalbert on the east coast of the Ards Peninsula. Furthermore, over half of the province's population live to the east of a line between Portrush and Newry, a region which occupies about one quarter of the province's total area (8530 square miles). Although the mileage of the bus routes in the western section is little different from that in the east, the daily frequency of its workings is less; 2–3 in certain areas of the west compared with 45–50 on some of the roads in the vicinity of Belfast. This discrepancy may be explained by lower industrial development in the west and the differences between the population densities on either side of the Portrush-Newry Line, viz 750 inhabitants per square mile in Fermanagh compared with 2100 in Down.

The growth and operation of the bus services in Ulster in the years previous to the formation of the NIRTB are described in this book. The first chapter gives a general background to the road services in the province. This is followed by chapters devoted to each of the companies subsequently known as the 'Big Five'; The Belfast and County Down Railway [BCDR], Great Northern Railway (Ireland) [GNR], Midland Railway, Northern Counties Committee [NCC], Belfast Omnibus Company [BOC], and HMS Catherwood Ltd. The seventh chapter contains short accounts of those companies which either had retained their independent status until the NIRTB take-over, or had gone out of business before the formation of this body. The two concluding chapters describe the services which were exempted from joining the NIRTB and the activities of those omnibus proprietors which were interested mainly in private-hire and touring. A brief mention is also made of the Coastal and Sureline privately owned buses which operated for several years between 1965 and 1985. There is also a list of all the operators which ran buses in Ulster between 1898 and 1935 and the compensation received by individual operators whose businesses were compulsorily acquired by the NIRTB in 1935.

Authors' Note

All buses and charabancs in service or within Northern Ireland on 27 August 1928 had to be registered. Applications had to state the name of the proprietor, the make, seating capacity and registration number of each vehicle together with the routes it intended to follow, time-table, mileage and a list of fares. These were all filed under the names of the individual owners and the terminals of the routes covered. Until the mid-1980s the files were available for public consultation in the Northern Ireland Public Record Office being catalogued under DEV7/109–195 (Operators) and DEV7/225–386 (Routes). Much of the detailed information about the services described in this book has been obtained from these files which, in recent years have not been available for consultation. As a result, the reference numbers of the appropriate DEV7 files have been deleted from the list of references quoted in this book.

Monetary values have been expressed in the currency of the period. Prior to 1970, the pound (£) was divided into 20 shillings, each of 12 pence – there being 240 old pennies to the £. One shilling corresponded to 5 new pence. The abbreviations used were 's' for shillings and 'd' for pence.

Distances have been expressed in the imperial system of miles and yards: 1 mile = 1.6 kilometres, 1 yard = 0.9144 metres.

In 1922 Ireland was partitioned into the Irish Free State whose government sat in Dublin, and Northern Ireland which had a local parliament based at Stormont, Belfast. The Irish Free State comprised the provinces of Leinster, Munster and Connacht and the three Ulster counties of Donegal, Cavan and Monaghan. Northern Ireland comprised the other six Ulster counties of Londonderry, Antrim, Down, Armagh, Tyrone and Fermanagh.

In 1949, under a new constitution, the Irish Free State became the Republic of Ireland.

1. Early Motor Buses and Charabancs

Throughout the twentieth century, fare paying passengers have been carried by mechanically propelled vehicles on the roads of Ulster. The early buses were primitive and their owners often men of limited finances but well endowed with initiative and not afraid to take risks, for in those days motors were a thoroughly unreliable novelty. Spectacular advances were made in motor transport during and after the 1914–18 War, so that by 1925 every town of importance in Ulster was served by a bus and by 1930 there was not a village, or clachan of houses, without a bus passing within convenient walking distance on at least one day each week.

Until the passing of the 1926 Northern Ireland Motor Vehicles Act only buses and their drivers needed to be licensed by the appropriate local authority. Under the act, however, the licensing of public service vehicles was transferred to the Ministry of Home Affairs and, after 27 August 1928, conductors, drivers, buses and the routes over which they worked had all to be licensed. Six of the principal operators anticipated the implications of this and merged to form the Belfast Omnibus Company in April 1927. During the next eight years the BOC expanded to become the largest bus owner in Ulster and, by 1935, owned about 170 of the 700 buses and charabancs regis-

4. BNCR Thornycroft steam bus outside the Belfast premises of Dublin based coachbuilders, Hutton, Sons & Co. The service began on 1 April 1902 between Greenisland station, Sea Park, Silverstream and Whiteabbey station. The vehicle was rebuilt as a lorry about 1909. W Montgomery Collection. UFTM L3882/9

5. Stirling bus at Rosapenna Hotel. These buses were fitted with 3 speed (and reverse) gearboxes and had a maximum speed of 14 mph. 'Seats were both comfortable and sanitary, having spring cushions covered with washable French leatherette. The large plate glass windows could be taken out in hot weather.' Ulster Museum, R Welch Collection. WO4/69/28

tered in Northern Ireland and annually carried over ten million passengers, which was about the same number as that conveyed by the railways within Northern Ireland. Furthermore, the act also led to a gradual reduction in the number of omnibus owners and private-hire operators.

The GNR and the NCC began to run buses in the early 1900s but they did little to expand this part of their activities until after the passing of the Northern Ireland Railway (Road Vehicles) Act of 1927. This eased the rigorous conditions under which railways had hitherto been permitted to operate road transport and gave them facilities somewhat similar to those enjoyed by private operators.

The trade depression of the early 1930s and the unrestricted competition between rail and road for traffic, especially freight, led the northern government to seek advice about its transport problems from Sir Felix J C Pole, the recently retired general manager of the Great Western Railway in England. The substance of his advice formed the basis of the Northern Ireland Road and Rail Act of 1935 in which the operation of all public road services, passenger and freight, came under the control of a public body known as the Northern Ireland Road Transport Board. In the autumn of the same year, all passenger-carrying public service operators, whether they ran buses on regular routes or provided coaches for tours and private-hire, were merged into the NIRTB, so that after 1 January 1936 there was one major operator for all passenger road services within Northern Ireland. Belfast Corporation and operators who worked trans-border services, such as the Londonderry and Lough Swilly Railway, were exempt. The omnibus fleet of the Great Northern Railway, which worked on both sides of the border, was divided, with the northern part being transferred to the NIRTB and the southern continuing under GNR ownership in the Free State.

The first mechanically-propelled public service buses in the province were the two steam omnibuses which the Belfast and Northern Counties Railway acquired in 1902 to convey passengers to and from its station at Greenisland. Another early service, but of a private nature, was provided by Lord Leitrim who obtained three 14-seater Scott-Stirling petrol omnibuses in 1903 to take guests from the railway station at Strabane to his hotel at Rosapenna, in County Donegal. In

6. Another of three Stirling buses which served the Rosapenna Hotel. The buses were numbered IH 2, IH 3 and IH 4 when vehicle registrations were begun in 1904. This photograph shows an outing of the Belfast Naturalists' Field Club in July 1903. The man with the cap and beard seated in the rear of the bus is William McKinney who was secretary of the Carnmoney Temperance Society. Ulster Museum, Welch Collection. WO4/69/22

7. Belfast Co-operative Society parade with two solid-tyred lorries temporarily converted for passengers' use. The banner on the second lorry reads 'Ireland's hope is in Co-operation'. Date, c1913. UFTM L1754/19

general, by the outbreak of the 1914–18 War, regular bus services were in operation in the Ards Peninsula and the northern shores of Lough Foyle, districts which were comparatively prosperous, but without rail facilities. On the other hand, motor charabancs had begun to run on short trips at seaside resorts, eg Henry McNeill's motors which provided a twice daily service on the Antrim Coast Road between Larne and Cushendall in 1911, Matthew Morrow's charabancs which began to run between Bangor and Donaghadee in the same year, and the Mourne Mountain Touring Company which brought charabancs to Warrenpoint in 1913. Another pre-war operator was Jacob O'Neill's Express Motor Company which advertised a scenic route between Belfast and Donaghadee via Helen's Bay, Crawfordsburn and the coast road from Bangor to Donaghadee.

In the years immediately following the 1914/18 War bus services developed rapidly throughout Ulster. Some of these were owned by proprietors, such as W Finlay of Castlewellan and J Poots of Waringstown, who had been running successful posting establishments for many years; others were the owners of well established family businesses and had obtained motor charabancs which they hired out for Sunday school and other outings. (In the horse-drawn era, the posting establishment was the equivalent of the present motor garage). In due course they discovered that there was money to be made by taking fare paying passengers to market in the nearest large town. Finally, many people had managed to scrape together sufficient money to pay a deposit on a bus, and then operate it as a family concern with the proprietor either driving or conducting himself. Furthermore, nearly all the more successful bus operators began by working from a smaller to a larger town, eg A Spence from Dromore to Belfast, HMS Catherwood from Maghera to Antrim and Belfast. The former became one of the founder members of the BOC and the latter continued as an independent operator until his take over by the NIRTB in 1935. By this time Catherwood had expanded to become the fourth largest bus operator (70 buses) in the province and was a member of the main board of Thomas Tilling, one of the largest transport holding companies in Britain.

2. Belfast and County Down Railway

The Belfast and County Down Railway opened a bus service between Newcastle and Kilkeel on 1 August 1916. Earlier in the same year, the railway and Norton & Co of Kilkeel had agreed to replace the Newcastle-Warrenpoint horse-car service by motor buses, the Nortons to work between Warrenpoint and Kilkeel and the BCDR between Kilkeel and Newcastle.[1] The railway immediately ordered three Dennis chassis from Charles Hurst of Belfast but, at the time, there was such a demand for motor vehicles for war service that the government would only release one chassis[2] and, on this, Hursts built a saloon body, the total cost of the vehicle coming to £1140. The bus made its 'press run' on 31 July[3] and went into service on 1 August 1916. It was based at Kilkeel and at first was restricted by fuel shortages to making only two round trips each day. When the war ended the frequency of the service was increased.

8. BCDR Dennis bus Reg IJ1538. The bus was operated on behalf of the BCDR by Norton & Co of Kilkeel, Co Down. Norton's manager, H A Matier wrote a letter to Dennis praising the vehicle's reliability, also saying that the driver deserves some credit for this as he is 'married to the car'. This publicity photograph was taken on 31 July 1916. UFTM L1529/10

9. BCDR Dennis bus Reg. 0I 5578 at Annalong. This bus operated between Newcastle and Kilkeel. Date, c1920. UFTM L1932/3

10. Ford Model T bus. This Co Down registered vehicle was owned by Norton's. The body was built by Massey Bros Coachbuilders, Wigan, England. UFTM L4079/7

Some two months before the arrival of the railway bus, Nortons took delivery of a 35 horse power Selden bus which had a grey body with seating for 16 passengers, the colour being chosen in the hope that it would not show up the dirt! Like several other motors of that era, its engine was equipped with two carburettors so that it could run on either petrol or paraffin.[4] It went into service on 23 May but wartime restrictions made it so difficult to get adequate fuel supplies, together with the imminent retirement of the Norton proprietor,[5] that the bus was sold to the railway for £450 on 8 September 1916.[6] It was then overhauled by J B Ferguson's garage in Belfast and painted in BCDR livery, after which it went into service between Newcastle and Kilkeel. In 1919 it was replaced by a 3-ton Dennis, the chassis for which had been obtained from Charles Hurst and the body built in the railway's own carriage shops; the original Dennis of 1916 remained on the road until 1923. Services between Newcastle and Kilkeel were greatly improved during the inter-war years when the route was worked by Leyland PLSC3 buses and nearly every train serving Newcastle connected with a bus for Kilkeel.

By the mid-1920s the full effect of uncontrolled road competition had become very serious and by May 1927 it was estimated that there were at least 27 bus services operating in BCDR territory.[7] The railway was at a distinct disadvantage, for many of the places served by it were much closer to Belfast by road than by rail. Thus Ballynahinch was 15 miles by road from the city compared with 22 miles by rail, and buses from this town, and those from Bangor, Holywood and Newtownards, were able to cross the River Lagan into Belfast city centre, whereas the company's trains terminated at Queen's Quay on the south bank of the river. Competition for the Ballynahinch traffic began in 1922 and that from Holywood and Newtownards two years later. At first the railway ignored the competition and then tried to meet it by reducing fares and, in some instances, running its own bus services. On 26 May 1927 the BCDR inaugurated its first post-war bus service which ran between Donaghadee and Ballywalter. Four return journeys were usually provided on weekdays with additional runs during holiday periods.

In May 1905, the BCDR, fearing an extension of the Belfast tramways to Holywood, began to run an additional 30 trains on weekdays between Belfast and Holywood, an action which enabled it to maintain its monopoly on this route until road competition began in 1924. By 1928, at least seven different bus operators, at one time or another, had competed for traffic on the route and single fares between Holywood and the city had been slashed to two old pennies. In the end the railway decided to meet this competition by buying out its rivals and putting its own buses on the route. The policy succeeded for, by 1930, only

11.BCDR Leyland PLSC1 bus Reg IJ 7816 with Leyland 31 seater body. This vehicle was new in 1926. Courtesy B Boyle. UFTM L3779/14

12. McClement's bus Reg XI 5327 at Sand Quay, Belfast in the late 1920s. This vehicle is an International. Courtesy J McClements. UFTM L892/2

one competitor was left, and the price of a single ticket had been restored to five old pennies. This high fare persuaded T Clements of Grove Street, Belfast to establish the Ulster Passenger Bus Combine which would enable the public to travel between Belfast and Holywood at fares less than those authorised by the government. Passengers would be charged a membership fee of 1s which would enable them to travel in any of the combine's buses by purchasing a 7d return ticket. It was claimed that, since passengers would be brought back to their starting points, his buses were really charabancs on tour and were exempt from fare regulations and the necessity of carrying conductors. The service was to have started on 29 September 1930 when the UPBC hoped to provide a quarter-hourly service between Belfast and Holywood. However, just before it began, the government ruled that it would be illegal for bus owners to charter buses to Clements for the operation of his scheme and, as the latter was unable to purchase the necessary buses, the project never came to fruition.

On 23 October 1928 the railway put its first bus (Leyland, 31-seater PLSC3) on the road between the Maypole, Holywood and Victoria Square, Belfast. Over the years the number of buses employed and the frequency of the services were both increased so that, ultimately, a railway bus departed from each terminal at ten minute intervals during weekdays.

In September 1924 Thomas McClements of Belfast began to compete for the Holywood-Belfast traffic. His first bus was a second-hand London General Omnibus which he had rebuilt as a single-decker. Initially he employed his brother as the driver and acted as conductor himself. Within a few years, he had increased his fleet

13. McClement's Tilling Stevens bus outside his office at 25 Oxford Street, Belfast in the late 1920s. Courtesy J McClements. UFTM L1308/8

of red and white buses to five, and was providing a quarter-hour service between Holywood and the city. Like many other early omnibus proprietors he was frequently in trouble with the authorities for overcrowding, for obstructing traffic by waiting too long at stops, and for exceeding the speed limit (12mph for solid tyred buses, 20mph for those with pneumatic tyres.) His response was to paper the windows and walls of his office at 25 Oxford Street, Belfast, with police court summonses.[8] Unfortunately, four of his buses were burnt on 28 October 1928, after which he tried to maintain a much reduced service with the aid of buses lent by other operators. However, by now he was in serious financial difficulties, and in May 1929, sold his business which consisted of three AEC buses for £1500 to the tour operator John Gaston of Templemore Avenue, Belfast. The latter had hoped to continue a quarter-hour service. However, after two months, Gaston decided to concentrate on private-hire and touring and in August sold the three buses to the railway for £2100.

14. Russell's Vulcan bus. In 1927 H Russell of Holywood was running five Vulcan buses in his fleet; four 20-seaters and one 32-seater. This photograph was taken at Oxford Street, Belfast in the late 1920s. UFTM L3237/12

Five months before the Gaston purchase, the BCDR acquired the service owned by H Russell of Holywood. This operator had obtained his first bus, a 20-seater Vulcan, in August 1926 and, within a year, his fleet had been augmented by three more 20-seater Vulcans and a 32-seater of the same make, which he used on a very intensive service between the Maypole in Holywood and Oxford Street in Belfast, a service which was maintained until he sold his buses to the railway in March 1929. The third operator to be taken over by the railway was S H Gillespie who, at one time had owned a tobacconist's shop in Holywood. In 1927 he acquired two 20-seater Reos which he used mainly for the provision of rush hour services until he sold them to the BCDR in August 1929. Four other bus owners – J Burton, J Clegg, McDonald and W F Nutt (Swift Service) – also provided short-lived intermittent services between Belfast and Holywood but which were never a very serious threat to those of the railway.

In November 1922 the BCDR began to give a small subsidy to the Pioneer Motor Service to run a winter bus service between the railway stations at Bangor and Donaghadee.[9] A few months later, the bus company agreed to accept tickets issued by the railway on its buses on this route. During subsequent years similar agreements were drawn up with other bus proprietors, namely Michael O'Reilly (Dromara-Ballynahinch), Sharvin Bros (Downpatrick-Strangford), J Patterson and W Huddleston the joint proprietors of the Ballykinlar MS (Downpatrick-Ballykinlar). In addition both the BCDR and GNR issued a Mourne Circular Tour in which patrons travelled by rail from Belfast to Newcastle with the BCDR, by bus from Newcastle to Warrenpoint, and returning by rail to Belfast with the GNR.

The BCDR had not the financial resources of either the NCC or the GNR and so was unable to buy for itself a transport monopoly in its territory. Thus it never ran buses between Belfast and Newtownards nor did it attempt to provide road services along the western shores of Strangford Lough. In 1935 its bus fleet consisted of 14 buses (6 Leyland, 6 Dennis, 2 Vulcan) all of which were painted in bluish green with the company's crest and name in full painted on their sides. Mudguards and wheels were usually black. The buses which first plied between Newcastle and Kilkeel were painted in the same shade of maroon as the company's coaching stock, with gold leaf lining and lettering. At the take over on 1 October 1935, the BCDR received 18792 NIRTB stocks for its bus services.

REFERENCES

1 BCDR Board Minutes: 5 April 1916
2 BCDR Board Minutes: 17 May, 6 June 1916
3 *Newry Reporter*: 3 August 1916
4 *Newry Reporter*: 23 May 1916
5 BCDR Board Minutes: 23 August 1916
6 BCDR Board Minutes: 19 September 1916
7 PRONI UTA/12/CGA/154
8 *Transport Topics* (Belfast): June 1927
9 BCDR Board Minutes: October/November 1922

3. Belfast Omnibus Company

15. BOC Daimler Charabanc Reg. XF 8161. This vehicle had either been purchased second-hand or was on hire. Date, c1927. UFTM L3785/5

The Belfast Omnibus Company was the largest omnibus operator in Ulster and, when it was absorbed into the Northern Ireland Road Transport Board on 1 October 1935, 169 buses were transferred to the new organisation. The BOC was first mooted in 1926 when some of the principal omnibus proprietors in the province realised that the financial prospects of their undertakings would soon become disastrous unless they could reduce the unlimited competition which was then prevalent on the roads. In April 1926 seven of them formed the North of Ireland Omnibus Company[1] and sought the advice of Henry C Merrett, a London accountant with wide experience of transport mergers. He came over to Ireland later in the year and by March 1927 informed the Northern Ireland Ministry of Commerce that nearly all the bus operators east of a line between Newry, Cookstown and Cushendall[2] would be willing to come into his proposed organisation. On 23 April of the same year the NIOC was superseded by the BOC which was incorporated as a public company on that day[3] and, two months later, on 27 June 1927, it became fully operational. During the next eight years over 40 bus owners joined the consortium, but HMS Catherwood and the three railway companies remained aloof and retained their separate identities until absorbed into the NIRTB on 1 October 1935. The seven founder members of the NIOC were; Ards MTC, Bangor MS, W Jellie, E Johnston, McKees MS Co, Smith Weatherup and McNeilly, and Spence and McCrea. E Johnston went out of business shortly afterwards, but the other six became founder members of the BOC.

The BOC's registered office was in London in premises shared with the Gresham Trust.[4] Three of its original directors were based in England – C W Batten, W H Capstick, C H Moller – and three came from Northern Ireland, namely W Jellie from Lisburn, S McLoughlin from Belfast, and M Morrow from Bangor. The total capital of the company, including a £100,000 debenture, was of the order of a quarter of a million pounds, which meant that throughout its working life it was severely under capitalised despite a cash injection of £75,500 received for the sale of its assets in counties Antrim, Derry and Tyrone to the NCC in 1930.

Advertisements for a rival organisation called the Ulster General Omnibus Company[5] appeared in the press a few weeks before the setting up of the BOC. This company was based in England

and its promoters, none of whom seem to have had any Irish connections, intended to raise £150,000 to operate a fleet of at least a hundred 'saloon buses' in the province but, as neither the financial press nor the investing public was interested, subscriptions were not forthcoming[6] and the project lapsed. One of the people closely associated with the scheme was an undischarged bankrupt named Henry Thomas Hart Spratt who, a few months previously, had persuaded a bus owner to join him in promoting a bus merger in England, but ended with his victim losing his buses and over £11,000 in cash. At the subsequent court hearing, the Registrar in Bankruptcy said that 'There are some people who could sell sand to the inhabitants of the Sahara and Hart Spratt is one of them.' In Ulster, several omnibus proprietors were charmed by him, including Edward Johnston of Ballynahinch, one of the seven founder members of the NIOC who parted with his buses in exchange for worthless cheques.[7]

The BOC operated mainly in Down but some of its buses also ran to parts of counties Antrim and Armagh where one of its routes in the latter county was extended through the Clogher Valley to Enniskillen, becoming the company's longest route, 93 miles. In its first three years the company also provided extensive services throughout parts of counties Antrim, Derry and Tyrone, but this part of its business was sold to the NCC on 26 March 1930, a transaction in which 59 buses and about 200 miles of bus routes became railway property and the BOC's route mileage was thereby reduced to 684 miles.

16. BOC AEC Regal bus with 34 seater body built by BOC. Seen here at the company's works when new in 1931. UFTM L3783/7

17. Karrier charabanc Reg OI A4 (a trade plate) at Sandhurst Road, Belfast opposite Chamber's Car factory c1919. The body was built by Chambers and the vehicle is fitted with their registration number. UFTM L1827/7

The company's local headquarters and its workshops were situated in University Street, Belfast in premises which had, at one time, been used by W & R Chambers to manufacture the only motor cars to have been designed and built on a commercial scale in Ireland before to the arrival of the De Lorean Car Company in 1981. It also had its own central bus terminal in Upper North Street, Belfast which opened in June 1928. Previous to this, buses had operated from the kerb side at different points in central Belfast. Thus, buses going in the Lisburn and Ballynahinch directions usually started from the Black Man Statue in College Square, Ormeau Avenue or Victoria Square and those going to Bangor and north Down collected their passengers in either Queen's Square or Oxford Street. After the opening of the terminal, local services continued to work from the Black Man, those going to Bangor and north Down went on using Queen's Square and Oxford Street and departures for all other places were concentrated on the new terminal in Upper North Street.

18. BOC buses at North Street depot, Belfast, 13 July 1931. Photographer A R Hogg. R Ludgate Collection. UFTM L1529/1

The majority of the company's services were based in Belfast, the three busiest routes being those going through Bangor, Lisburn and Newtownards, on which between 45 and 60 double workings were provided on weekdays. (Double working is a round trip or a return journey – ie to a destination and back to the starting point). Nearly all Lisburn buses travelled over the main road through Dunmurry, with a few being routed either via Hillhall or Suffolk. All buses for Bangor went through Holywood and then ran either via Clandeboye or via Crawfordsburn. Dromara, in the centre of County Down, could be reached either via Lisburn (six double workings taking 75 minutes) or via Ballynahinch (three double workings in 65 minutes). Newcastle had eight double workings from Belfast, some being routed via Ballynahinch, Spa and Castlewellan and the others via Seaforde (near Tullymurry) and Dundrum. There were also eight double workings between Belfast and Armagh and ten to Newry, the latter being allowed 1 hr 50 min for the 38-mile journey. Local services were also provided to and from all the principal market towns in County Down and parts of north Armagh. Villages in the neighbourhood of Belfast were not neglected, thus Crumlin had twelve double workings to the city, some going via Lisburn and the others via Hannahstown. There were at least three double workings to Ballygowan, two of which terminated in country districts a few miles beyond the village. One of these ran to Florida Manor and carried the name FLORIDA on its destination blind, a name which may have caused envy among the

19. BOC ADC bus Reg XI 9345 at Gilford, Co Down, c1930. Photographer A R Hogg. Courtesy B Boyle. UFTM L3784/10

inhabitants of the Castlereagh Road in Belfast when they saw a bus labelled for sunny Florida passing their homes on wet winter evenings. Sunday services, with a frequency of about a third of that operated on weekdays, were usually provided throughout the year and, during the summer, additional buses would run from inland towns such as Armagh to the seaside on Sunday afternoons.

Passengers holding ordinary single tickets were charged about 1d per mile with returns being available at a slightly lower mileage rate. Cheap day returns, and weekend tickets were also issued and weekly 'Run-About' tickets could be purchased which gave their holders unlimited travel over all BOC routes for 15s. The company also provided a cheap and expeditious parcel service,

20. BOC Dennis Ace parcels van Reg CZ 4972. One of a number of this type of van operated by the company. Date, 1934. R Ludgate Collection. UFTM L3773/5

parcels being conveyed to any company agency in the province at a rate based only on weight, thus a 7lb. parcel cost 4d. and one weighing 56lbs. 1s 6d; an additional 2d. per parcel was charged for delivery to any address within a mile of a depot or agency. The latter were established in every village through which the company's buses passed, the agents being usually small shopkeepers, in whose premises parcels could be left and prospective passengers wait for their buses when the weather was inclement. In addition, the company had depots manned by its own staff in the larger towns, eg Bangor and Fivemiletown.

The BOC was an amalgamation made up from about 40 individual operators and, during its eight years as an independent organisation, was gradually becoming an efficient, well knit, body. It was fortunate in its general manager, James McCrea and its chief engineer James Courtney. The former had been a partner with A Spence of Dromore and had been mainly responsible in bringing together the seven operators which formed the NIOC in 1926. He became the first resident manager of the BOC and was also the first general manager of the NIRTB. He was always highly respected by those who had worked with him, but unfortunately died shortly after taking up the appointment. McCrea was a good friend of Matthew Morrow and once a year they went on a luxury bus trip around Ireland with other members of the BOC – a busman's holiday! James Courtney had been one of the proprietors of McKee's Motor Service Company Ltd which had been established in 1924 to run buses between Belfast and Whitehead. He was a most competent engineer with a flair for innovation. Thus, in the 1930s, he modified some bus engines to run on the oil which had been a waste by-product in the distillation of coal tar in the Belfast Corporation Gas Works. A bus fitted with one of these modified engines made a successful press trip[8] from Belfast to the Mournes on 6 July 1931 but, when the accountants found that the substantial savings in fuel costs had been more than totally absorbed in increased maintenance charges, the experiments were stopped. Courtney spent the greater part of his working life with buses and ultimately became the chief engineer of the NIRTB. The first general manager of the company was H C Merrett, who had played a leading role in getting it established, but he returned to England within a few months of his taking up the appointment. However, he resumed his connection with the province in 1932 when he became one of the Thomas Tilling nominees on the board of HMS Catherwood.[9]

Until the passing of the 1926 Northern Ireland Motor Vehicles Act[10] only buses and their drivers needed to be licensed by the local authority. Under this act, the licensing of public service vehicles was transferred to the Ministry of Home Affairs and, after 27 August 1928, conductors, drivers, buses, time tables and routes had all to be licensed by this government department. This, together with regulations published by the government as a consequence of the Belfast Bus War, meant that no new bus service could be started over a route on which an operator was already providing an adequate and satisfactory service; hence, in practice, the only way in which a proprietor could expand his business was to buy up existing services. The BOC followed this policy and continued to grow, so that by the autumn of 1935 it owned about a quarter of the 700 buses which were, at that time, licensed in Northern Ireland; at the take over the company received 390291 NIRTB stocks for its total assets, which included 169 buses.

In its early years the BOC was seriously handicapped by having to operate at least 16 different makes of bus, many of which had been allowed to get into a deplorable mechanical condition due to the neglect of their previous owners. However, during its short life, it took steps to enforce routine maintenance and other sound workshop practices, and had restricted, as far as possible, the purchase of new buses to ADCs and AECs, so that by 1935 it owned over a hundred of the former, the majority of which had been purchased by 1932. Until 1929 the bodies of all new BOC buses had been built by English builders such as Hall Lewis and Christopher Dodson but, after

21. BOC AEC Regent double decker bus Reg. AZ 7388 outside the company's offices in Belfast. Supplied new in 1931 with 50 seater body by Shorts. Courtesy B Boyle. UFTM L3783/11

the opening of the company's own body shop in Belfast, all single deck bodies were built locally. In 1931 the company obtained the first of its eight 52-seater low-bridge double-deckers; the first five had bodies built by Shorts on AEC Regent chassis and the remainder, obtained a year later, had bodies built by Weymann. Initially its buses were painted brown and white with black mudguards and wheels but, because of the similarity of this livery to that of the NCC, the colour scheme was altered to green and white in 1930.

Brief historical accounts of many of the operators who became members of the BOC are given out later in this chapter, and the names of all who joined it between 1927 and 1935 are included in Appendix C.

22. BOC buses on display at the Balmoral Show, Belfast, 29 May 1930. It is said that the recipient of the brochure is their rival Mr HMS Catherwood. Photographer A R Hogg. Courtesy B Boyle. UFTM L3784/11

North Down

The first motor bus on the roads of north Down made its inaugural run on 25 October 1907. On that afternoon the 12-seater, 16 horse power, Albion charabanc, belonging to the Irish Motor Transport Company of Edinburgh, set off from Newtownards with a distinguished company on board and arrived in Portaferry, some 20 miles away, about an hour and a quarter later.[1] Its owners had intended to provide two round workings daily and advertised that their passengers would be carried in 'covered cars, comfortably upholstered and fully protected from the weather,'[2] and that the single fare would be 2s. However, after a few weeks the bus was taken off the road as it had encountered difficulties in 'surmounting the braes en route.'[3] The defect must have been remedied for, although there is no report of its return to regular service, the *Newtownards Chronicle* of 11 April 1908 states, that at the Ballyhaft horse races, 'the green motor car of the Irish Motor Transport Company had a busy day' and goes on to say that the vehicle was driven by John Montgomery.

At the beginning of 1908 the Newtownards-Portaferry service was revived by the Reliance Motor Service,[4] a company which was associated with Arthur Stringer who, at the time, was also manager of the Station Cab Company, one of the largest public carriers in Belfast. Today, the No.10 Service of Ulsterbus runs over the route first worked by the Reliance MS thereby making it the oldest continuously used motor bus route in Ireland. Shortly after this Norton & Co, who had been carrying the mail between Newtownards and

23. Reliance *Dennis charabanc Reg OI 289 at the Royal Hotel, Quay Street, Bangor c1908. The service ran from Bangor to Donaghadee via the Seacliff Road as Ballymagee Street, (now High Street) was too steep for the vehicles to climb. UFTM L3261/8*

24. Reliance *Thornycroft charabanc at the Nugent Arms Hotel, Portaferry about 1915. Photographer W A Green. UFTM WAG 613*

Portaferry in two-horse four-wheeled brakes since the 1850s, withdrew from the service, after which the contract to carry the mail was given to J B Ferguson and Hugh Graham.[5] The former owned a garage in Chichester Street, Belfast, and the latter was the proprietor of a posting establishment in North Street, Newtownards. In March 1908 they took delivery of a double-decker Milnes-Daimler motor omnibus which had been specially designed for the service. The bus was scheduled to leave Belfast at 0600 hrs and, after calling at Newtownards Post Office at 0700 hrs, was due in Portaferry at 0900 hrs; on the return journey it departed from Portaferry at 1600 hrs. Its arrival meant that now there were three double workings each weekday between Newtownards and Portaferry, one being provided by the Royal Mail and two by the Reliance M.S. This pattern did not change when James O'Brien of Portavogie replaced Hugh Graham in 1911 as one of the joint contractors for the mail.[6] At the time

25. Motor charabanc Reg OI H2 at Main Street, Bangor, Co Down c1908. This registration was a trade plate registered to J B Ferguson Ltd., in Chichester Street, Belfast. The horse-drawn vehicle belonged to H Graham. (Valentine Postcard). UFTM L3235/4

O'Brien, was the owner of a posting establishment at Portavogie and had been running horse-drawn cars between this town and Newtownards. In June 1914 he took delivery of a 30-seater double decked bus which he named *Pride of Ulster*. It was one of the first buses in the British Isles in which the passenger accommodation could be heated during the winter.[7] Its first driver was Bob Bunyan who was brought over from England as it was believed that no local man would be capable of driving such a large machine.[8]

In 1915 Stringer sold the Reliance M.S. to Frank Hamilton of Portaferry who had been one of the drivers of the Royal Mail.[9] In September 1916 Hamilton combined with David Hutchinson, Thomas Somerset and James O'Brien to form the Ards Motor Transport Co Ltd.[10] At the time Hutchinson and Somerset were among the leading mill owners in Ireland and had several linen mills in north Down to which many of the operatives were conveyed each day in buses

26. Reliance *Thornycroft double-decker bus at the Nugent Arms Hotel, Portaferry, Co Down c1912. Courtesy W Montgomery. UFTM L3882/8*

belonging to Hamilton and O'Brien. However, there were so many complaints about high fares and general unreliability that the mill owners decided to provide their own transport. After a

27. Stringer's Reliance *Thornycroft double-decker bus Reg OI 694 in Conway Square, Newtownards, c1912. Courtesy R MacDonald. UFTM L2148/6*

28. The Pride of Ulster *Milnes-Daimler bus Reg IJ 968 at BCDR Newtownards railway station, Co Down in May 1914. The 30-seater body was built by H Hora Ltd, 36a Peckham Road, London, for the Portavogie owner at a cost of £400. Heating for passengers was provided by exhaust-heated radiators under the seats. UFTM L1527/9*

few months they realised that it would probably be more satisfactory if the transport of their employees was carried out by a separate organisation and, on their initiative, the Ards MT Co Ltd was formed. The new company's activities expanded rapidly and, by 1919, it was not only working to Portaferry via Kircubbin and via Portavogie, but also running between Newtownards and Donaghadee via Bangor. The company ceased running between Bangor and Donaghadee in the early 1920s but continued to work from Newtownards to Bangor and to Portaferry until it became part of the BOC in 1927. By this time its buses were providing 15 double workings between Newtownards and Bangor via Conlig, 10 from Belfast to Portaferry (some via Ballywalter, others via Kircubbin) as well as a local service between Ballywalter and Donaghadee.

29. *Ards Motor Transport Company's* The All British *McCurd bus, August 1916. This bus was owned by Frank Hamilton of Portaferry and carried both mail and passenger traffic. The body was built by J B Ferguson of Belfast. UFTM L2058/9*

30. Ards Motor Transport Co Ltd. Karrier bus at the Custom House, Belfast, c1926. The body was painted primrose yellow and may have been built by Pantridge of Dromore. The man standing in the centre is John Eadie. UFTM L2057/8

The early buses belonging to the company were fitted with solid tyres and had an entrance platform at their rear from which an outside stair led to the roof. The latter was fitted with side-boards to facilitate the storage of baggage and market produce and, when the bus was full, some of the younger male passengers would travel on the roof. Several of the early buses had their front mudguards replaced by stout metal shelves so that heavy articles, such as pig carcasses, could be secured to these for their journey to market in Newtownards. Many of the company's buses were fitted with Karrier engines and had primrose yellow bodies carrying the title Ards Motor Transport Co Ltd, on their sides.

The Ards MTC had only one competitor on the road between Newtownards and Portaferry. This was the Moss Line which had been started by A J Moss of Newtownards in 1920 using a former London General Omnibus which he painted maroon.[11] Shortly afterwards he obtained two charabancs, both of which he painted green and named *Erin's Isle*. In 1923 he acquired a 32-seater Leyland charabanc, which was reputed to have been the first public service motor in the Ards to have pneumatic tyres.[12] In February 1925 his buses followed the lead set by the Ards MTC in the previous year, and extended all their workings by running on from Newtownards to Belfast.[13] In the next year Moss expanded his business by the purchase of the two small Lancia buses with which John Eadie and William Torney of Newtownards had begun their Lancia Bus Service in 1925. This service had initially provided seven double workings between Newtownards and Belfast[14] and was very popular, especially with police recruits training at the Royal Ulster Constabulary depot in the town. Its proprietors had originally been drivers with the Ards MTC[15] before starting their own company and continued to drive for Moss after he had taken over their business in 1926, finally ending their driving days with Ulsterbus.

Ever since the mid-1920s the road between Newtownards and Belfast has been well provided with public transport. In the mid-1920s six operators (Ards MTC, Kane Bros, Lancia B S, Moss Line, John McCartney's Pioneer Buses and the Imperial B S) competed for this traffic. This was at a time when the single fare to Belfast was often reduced to 6d (9d return) and when passengers were intensely loyal to their favourite operator, and would wait patiently for *their* bus to come along, even when this meant that several rivals had to pass during their wait. To help patrons identify their buses by night, coloured lights were sometimes carried. The Imperial B S used blue lights and Eadie and Torney green. By the end of 1927 the Ards MTC, as well as the Lancia and Moss Line buses, had all been merged into the BOC, thereby reducing the number of operators on the road between Newtownards and Belfast to four. Together these provided a minimum of 45 double workings on weekdays and 13 on Sundays, until the absorption by the NIRTB. To this day, a high frequency service has been continued over this route.

The first bus to ply between Newtownards and Bangor may possibly have started in the autumn of 1907. On 30 November of that year the *Newtownards Chronicle* advertised that a thrice daily bus service between the two towns was about to start; but as this was to be worked by the

31. The crew of the Bangor Queen *bus which ran between Belfast and Bangor. The driver and conductor have stopped for a break at the Sand Quay, Belfast. UFTM L4079/8*

Albion bus, which had already proved itself to be unreliable on the road to Portaferry, it is probable the service never got under way. Nine years later the Ards MTC began to run a bus between Newtownards, Bangor and Donaghadee for the convenience of operators engaged in war work at Hutchinson and Somersets mills in the area.[16] The Bangor – Donaghdee section of this service was withdrawn at the end of the 1914–18 War but the Ards MTC continued to run between Newtownards and Bangor via Conlig despite severe competition from local horse and motor car owners as well as the arrival of Morrow's buses on the same route. The latter were owned by Matthew Morrow whose family had been

32. Bangor Queen *Vulcan bus owned by McKinstry & McCready, c1927. The photo was taken in Southport where Vulcans were made. It had a low chassis which allowed for easy boarding by passengers. Courtesy B Boyle. UFTM L3782/16*

33. *Enterprise Dennis charabanc Reg CM 364 at the Sand Quay, Belfast. It had canvas side screens to protect passengers from the elements. Date, 1923. Courtesy W J Patterson. UFTM L3723/2*

operating a posting establishment in Bangor since 1885. On 1 December 1911 his company was incorporated as the Bangor Motor Service Company Ltd with Matthew Morrow, himself, as chairman and managing director.[17] In the summer of the same year he had started running motor charabanc trips from Bangor and also to operate a Dennis charabanc between Bangor and Donaghadee. In 1919 he started a service to Newtownards but five years later he gave up this service, as well as that to Donaghadee, and on 1 June 1924 began to run buses between Bangor and Belfast,[18] a route on which he competed with the trains of the BCDR and, from 10 June 1925, with the maroon Bangor Queen buses. These were owned by McKinstry and McCready but, by mid-1927, had gone out of service. Morrow's buses better known as the Enterprise Bus Service usually worked between the Esplanade in Bangor and Oxford Street in Belfast and, by the mid-1920s, was maintaining a half hourly service during the summer months. Enterprise buses were painted grey and were garaged in Holborn Avenue. The company's office was in Quay Street in Bangor. In

34. *Enterprise AEC bus Reg. IJ 6051. The destination board reads Bangor-Belfast via Clandeboye. Date, 1923. Courtesy W J Patterson. UFTM L1528/4*

1926 it was involved with six other operators in the formation of the NIOC and, in April 1927, became one of the founder members of the BOC when Matthew Morrow was given a seat on the board of the new organisation.[19] However, there seems to have been a considerable amount of in-fighting on the board and in September Morrow resigned. Shortly afterwards, he, and his son, became substantial shareholders in the Gordon Bus Service which ran buses between Dublin and Cavan.

Immediately on taking over the working of the Belfast-Bangor services from the Enterprise buses on 27 June 1927, the BOC vigorously continued the challenge of competing with the trains of the BCDR for the major share of this traffic. By so doing, it dominated the road so successfully that only one competitor ever dared to compete against it. This was a 20-seater Dennis bus advertised as 'COB' – Clegg's Own Bus – which ran for a few weeks in the late summer of 1927, its passengers paying 9d and 1s for a single or return journey. This was the first occasion on which it was possible to purchase a return ticket for a journey by land between the two places at a fare as low as a shilling. Within a short time both BCDR and BOC were issuing shilling day return tickets, the former advertising the service as 'Bangor and Back for a Bob.'

The BOC usually provided a quarter-hour service throughout the greater part of the day but at holiday peak periods buses would leave either terminal as soon as they were loaded. The BOC also provided a frequent service between Bangor and Newtownards via Conlig and on 14 October 1928 the Tonic Buses also began to work between the towns over an indirect route via the Six Road Ends. However, a month later the two operators came to the agreement that the BOC would provide a weekday service of 17 round workings via Conlig and the Tonic bus service 13 via the Six Road Ends.

Only one other operator in the Bangor area joined the BOC. This was James Coey who owned the Viking Auto Service which, in the late 1920s, was providing ten double workings between Bangor and Donaghadee during the summer months and, in winter, ran between Bangor railway station and Ward Avenue in the town. However, in September 1929 he sold his two 14-seater buses (Crossley; Overland) to the BOC.

Lisburn, Lurgan and Armagh

During the summer of 1924 Spence's Auto Service, the Classic and the Violet Bus Services were all running over the road between Lisburn and Belfast and continued on this run until all three were merged as the BOC in the spring of 1927.

The first of these was Spence's A S which was owned by Alexander Spence and James McCrea, both of whom were the proprietors of successful retail shops in Dromore, County Down. Their first bus, a 36-seater AEC with solid tyres, was described in the local press as being like an 'hotel lounge on wheels'. It was named the *Ulster Queen* and was painted in the bluish purple livery which became standard for all the Spence buses. It set off on its first commercial run from the Market Square in Dromore at 0930 hrs on Wednesday, 10 December 1923 and arrived at the Black Man statue in Belfast an hour later.[1] Initially two double workings were provided daily but this frequency was increased to five on weekdays and two on Sundays with the addition of the *Northern Queen* three months later. In December 1924, some of the company's Belfast – Dromore workings were extended to Banbridge.[2]

35. Ulster Queen *AEC bus with both fore and aft entrance-exit doors for passengers; its solid tyres made it subject to a 12 mph speed limit. R Ludgate Collection. UFTM L4079/2*

36. The Wee Queen *was fitted with pneumatic tyres allowing it to be driven at 20 mph max. R Ludgate Collection. UFTM L4079/3*

Competition soon became very keen and, at times, the single fare for the 17 miles from Dromore to Belfast would be reduced to 6d with the additional inducement that on Sundays workmen would be carried free. The Spence AS had not only to face three rival bus owners on the road between Dromore and Lisburn but had also, at one time or another, to face competition from over a dozen operators on the main road between Lisburn and Belfast. Therefore, it is not surprising that Spence and McCrea were well aware of the financial hazards of unbridled competition and were among those who initiated the moves which led to the formation of the BOC in 1927. Their company owned seven buses (6 AEC; 1 Lancia) which were all named after Queens and were frequently advertised[3] as 'The Aristocrats of Busdom.'

37. The Violet *Maudslay, 35 seater bus owned by James Crothers and Alexander Dugan. The body was built in Dromore by Thomas Pantridge & Sons who ran a coachbuilding business. Date, c.1926 Courtesy Mrs M M^c^Kinney. UFTM L4079/10*

The Classic Bus Service was owned by William Jellie of Railway Street, Lisburn, who was a man of substance with an extensive posting and undertaking business, as well as being the proprietor of several other commercial ventures in the town. By September 1924 his buses, mainly AECs, were providing 10 double workings between Lisburn and Belfast, the eight-mile journey being timed to take about half an hour. A year later, some of his buses began to run to the city of Armagh, a route on which he had considerable competition from the Criterion buses which also ran between Belfast and the Cathedral City. Jellie himself was one of seven operators involved in the formation of the NIOC in 1926 and later became one of the first three Northern Ireland directors of the BOC.

The Violet Bus Service was started by James Crothers and Alexander Dugan of Lisburn in 1924, their first bus being a 35-seater Maudslay which, like all other Violet buses, had its body built by E J Pantridge of Dromore. It was painted violet and had violet curtains, the reason for the name and the colour being that Mrs Crothers, who was a gifted artist, had just painted a bunch of violets when she was asked to suggest a name for her husband's bus service.[4] The company's first bus ran between Dromara and Belfast but its main interest was soon concentrated on the road between Lisburn and Belfast where, in June 1926, it was providing 28 double workings on weekdays, the first bus leaving Lisburn at 0730 hrs and the last returning from Belfast at 2230 hrs; on Sundays 14 double workings were provided. By this time the workings to Dromara had been reduced to two on weekdays. One of the company's owners, James Crothers, was also a hardware merchant but, when his bus company joined the BOC in 1927, he became a full time officer of the new organisation and ultimately became the Traffic Superintendent of the NIRTB. In this capacity he supervised the wartime evacuations from Belfast when thousands of people were moved to safety out of the city within a few hours. On 8 December 1944 he became a war casualty himself, being killed in a road accident when on duty in the vicinity of Antrim.[5]

At least six other operators living in the Lisburn area joined the BOC. The first was Henry Courtney who formerly owned three Lancia buses which he named *Britannia's Pride, Erin's Pride* and *Ulster's Pride* and used them on an intensive service between Lisburn and Belfast via Hillhall. By the time his company was acquired by the BOC, his buses had been experiencing severe competition from the Cosy Bus Service which was owned by Maxwell and McClean of Hillhall and provided 14 double workings over the same nine mile route between Lisburn and Belfast. The Cosy BS had not the financial resources to survive the long struggle, in which the single fare to Belfast was finally reduced to 6d, and so went out of business in September 1928 when its two buses were taken off the road. George Gillespie began to run the *Lisnagarvey Queen* between Ravernet, Sprucefield and Belfast in the mid-1920s and joined the BOC in the summer of 1927. Later in the same year, Scott and McGregor (whose bus, the *Wee McGregor*, had been running for a few months between Dromara and Belfast via Lisburn) also joined the BOC as did Buchanan and Cunningham who operated the Rosevale Bus Service between Broomhedge and Belfast. The last was Mrs Elizabeth G Martin (see page 28) who seems to have been something of a 'Bus Owning Nomad'. At various times she had run buses between Ballynahinch and Belfast, had competed against the trams within Belfast city boundary, and had operated a bus service with four double workings between Belfast and Drumbo which she transferred to the BOC in 1927. Three years later the BOC purchased the goodwill of a service between Dromara and Belfast which had been started by E & F Spence of Hillsborough in May 1928. This service had been designed to undercut the fares charged by the BOC, but it was so unreliable that the Ministry of Home Affairs cancelled its operating licence which was subsequently given to the BOC. Two operators, Thomas Morgan and Martha Chambers were taken over in 1931. The former had run two 20-seater buses (Reo; Thornycroft) which traded as the Duchess Bus Service, between Donacloney and Belfast, some workings being routed via The Maze and the others via Hillsborough and Flatfield. The Chambers service had been started by Samuel Chambers of Lambeg in the mid-1920s with a working between Lisburn and Ballyskeagh. This was extended to Belfast after his acquisition of a second bus which Thomas McKee had been running between Ballyskeagh and Belfast. Shortly after the transaction, Mr Chambers died and his widow took over his business but, after a few months, sold it, together with a 20-seater Renault bus, to the BOC.

38. Master McGrath *Thornycroft bus Reg XI 5221, named after a famous racing greyhound from the area. The service was owned by Mrs Sarah Cummins. Date, 13 June 1926. Courtesy Mr Osborne. UFTM L916/3*

The Balmoral, the Criterion and Cummin's buses all passed through Lisburn on their way from north Armagh to Belfast. The Balmoral buses were the property of C McAfee, who lived on the Lisburn Road in Belfast, and began to run buses between Belfast and Lurgan in 1925, and the owners of the Criterion buses came from Armagh. Both these companies were merged into

39. Welcome *AEC bus Reg. XI 4219, 1925. Pictured from left, J Edgar, Mrs Sarah Cummins, Jack Cummins, D McKerry. UFTM L3788/5*

the BOC in 1927. However, by this time, Mrs Sarah Cummin, who had owned a 24-seater Thornycroft which she called *Master McGrath* and a 32-seater AEC named *Welcome,* had retired from the road on which she had begun to operate between Lurgan and Belfast in 1925. From all accounts[6] she, and her service, were not lacking in character and it is claimed that she often employed her daughters Daisy and Violet as conductors. Furthermore, one of her drivers was reputed to have driven the 20 miles from Lurgan to Belfast in 25 minutes (the journey should have taken over an hour if observing the speed limit), after which he emigrated to drive buses in Glasgow.

The first buses to run in Portadown were owned by Henry Brook of Stranraer and John Hodge of Galashiels who formed H Brook & Co (Ireland) Ltd[7] in 1924 and, in the next year reconstituted their company[8] as the Six Counties Motor Co Ltd. They appointed N W Brodie as their local manager and acquired four buses (2 AECs and 2 Berliets) which provided services to Donacloney, to Banbridge and, in 1927, a short-lived service between Derry, Strabane and Sion Mills. They also owned an AEC charabanc with which they ran excursions to Warrenpoint and summer evening trips to Maghery on Lough Neagh.[9] However, they did not forget the attractions of Scotland[10] and during the summer of 1926 organised day trips on which their patrons went by rail to Larne, where they boarded the steamer for Stranraer. On arrival at Stranraer they were taken in one of Brook's Scottish charabancs to Ballantrae and then sailed for home on the evening steamer, being due home in Portadown just before midnight, their trip having cost them 25s, which included First Class travel throughout but no meals. The company usually advertised under the heading 'The Pilot' and many of its advertisements contained the phrases 'We were the pioneers of cheap travel. We still lead, others follow.' In November 1927, the company joined the BOC after which Mr Brodie, its local manager, who seems to have been a part-time employee, was able to spend more of his time looking after his own buses which were working in the Cookstown area. (See page 98.)

Mid-Down

The BOC was particularly strong in mid-Down where, by 1935, it had secured a monopoly of the Belfast-Newcastle, the Belfast-Downpatrick and the Belfast-Killyleagh traffic. Its busiest route was that between Belfast and Ballynahinch, a road on which, between 1922 and the formation of the NIRTB in 1935, the BOC had to face at least eight other operators.[1] Elsewhere in mid-Down bus services were provided by at least twelve separate operators, all of whom had either gone out of business or had joined the BOC by 1935.

The first mid-Down omnibus proprietor was Edward Johnston of Ballynahinch who acquired a second-hand London General Omnibus[2] which he put on the road in June 1922 (see page 30). Toward the end of the year he augmented his fleet with two charabancs, which he named *Leader and Follow,* and took a full page advertisement in the *Belfast and Ulster Directory* in which he stated the Johnston Omnibus Service would provide four double workings each weekday between Ballynahinch and Victoria Square in Belfast, the single fare being 2s. In September 1923 the first of his serious rivals came onto the road. This was J Harrison of the Ballynahinch Motor Service, who worked five round trips over the same route and, like Johnston, also extended some of these to the Spa, Dromara and Drumaness; but whereas Johnston subsequently ran some buses to Newcastle, Harrison's services never went beyond Drumaness. The latter also took a full page advertisement in the Belfast directory but, after a few years, he got into financial difficulties[3] with the suppliers of his buses (AEC) and was declared a bankrupt in January 1927. Within six months, Johnston was also insolvent. Early in 1927 he had come under the spell of an undischarged bankrupt named Hart Spratt of the dubious Ulster General Omnibus Company who had intended to merge some of the smaller operators with his organisation.[4] He got possession of Johnston's buses but, before handing over a cheque for the £8000 which had been the agreed price, he borrowed an additional £1400 from Johnston and then disappeared. He re-appeared next year in a north London court where he received a twelve month sentence.[5]

In March 1924 David McAtee of Kilkeel began a bus service between his home town and Belfast, and in 1926, the Edgar Brothers[6] of Belfast also began a rival service between the same two places, which traded under the name of the Phantom Bus Service. Since all the Kilkeel buses went through Ballynahinch, their presence increased the frequency of the service on the road from Ballynahinch to the city. The Edgars joined the BOC in April 1928 but McAtee continued as an independent operator until March 1933 when he, too, was absorbed into the BOC.

40. Edgar's Bus Service which ran from 1926 to 1928 in direct competition with McAtees. Edgar's buses joined with BOC in April 1928. Courtesy B Boyle. UFTM L3782/7

On 29 October 1925 Mrs Elizabeth Martin (see page 25), who at that time was living in Belfast, began to run buses between Belfast and Ballynahinch and continued to operate over the route until June 1928 when she moved some of her buses to take part in the Belfast Bus War. During her time as an omnibus proprietor Mrs Martin carried on a vendetta with the Public Service Vehicle Inspectorate concerning the condition of her buses. Her arrival intensified the competition on the Belfast-Ballynahinch road and led to an increase in the services to over 50 double workings and a decrease in fares for the 15 mile journey to 9d single and 1s return.

The last operator to go onto the road arrived in January 1927. This was Thomas Spence who owned a fish and chip restaurant in Belfast and was the proprietor of the Triumph Motor Service. He used mainly Vulcan 28/32-seater buses which were painted blue and carried a blue light to assist their customers in identifying them at night. In August of the same year he expanded his business by opening a new service between Belfast and Florida Manor via Ballygowan, a route on which he usually provided three double workings; whereas on the Ballynahinch road he maintained a minimum of 14 round trips daily, all of which ran on to either Drumaness, Edendariff or the Spa. Spence seems to have been keen on punctuality for his advertisements usually contained the phrase 'Will patrons please note that the buses leave Ballynahinch at local time[7] which is five minutes in advance of Belfast time.' (On the instructions of the local lord of the manor who was habitually late, the town clock was always set five minutes fast, so that he knew he would catch the train.) Furthermore, Spence's timetable handouts were generally headed 'Support your local carrier' and 'The man who kept fares down.' The latter was no idle boast, for as soon as he had sold out to the BOC in May 1930, the single fare from Ballynahinch to Belfast was increased from 9d to 1s 4d.

During the 1920s Michael O'Reilly, who owned a posting establishment and several other business ventures in Dromara, began to run a twice daily bus service to connect with the trains at Ballynahinch station. After a short time, the BCDR arranged to issue tickets from any of its stations to Dromara which would be good for travel by O'Reilly's Dromara Mail Motor Service from Ballynahinch, a through facility which continued until O'Reilly joined the BOC in 1927.

The first bus service between Downpatrick and Belfast was started by Atchinson Moffett of Downpatrick[8] in March 1923. Two years later his Downpatrick Motor Service sold out to W J McCurdy of Belfast and William Nevin of Crossgar. By the end of 1926, the new owners were providing six double workings between Downpatrick and Belfast and, during the summer of that year, had also begun a regular service between Downpatrick and Ardglass. This was the first bus service to Ardglass which, hitherto, had only been visited by the occasional bus from Downpatrick on Sunday afternoons. In the summer of the next year McCurdy and Nevin joined the BOC which continued to provide a similar type of service to Belfast. An alternative bus route between Downpatrick and Belfast, which went via Killyleagh and Crossgar, was opened by J Morris of Downpatrick[9] in November 1927, but it seems to have lasted for only a few weeks. However, a biweekly service was revived again between Killyleagh and Crossgar by the BOC in 1929 when two double workings were provided on Tuesdays and Thursdays.

In May 1933 Downpatrick became a BOC preserve when the company took over the two Vulcan charabancs which the Sharvin brothers had been running between Strangford and Downpatrick. The Sharvins, who had owned a posting business in Strangford since before the turn of the century, obtained their first motor bus in March 1920.[10] In its early days it ran in competition with a motor charabanc belonging to H F Quayle who had an interest in the ferries which plied between Strangford and Portaferry. Quayle obtained his vehicle in October 1919 but only kept it on the road for about 18 months.[11] In 1923 the Conway brothers, who also owned a posting business in Strangford, set up the Strangford Motor Service

41. Sharvin's bus outside Sharvin's Shop, the Square, Strangford, Co Down. Driver/conductor Johnny Curran posed beside vehicle. Date, 1920s. Photographer W A Green. UFTM WAG 2744

which provided four trips daily compared with the eight runs made by the Sharvin buses, the buses of each proprietor being scheduled to cover the 8 miles to Downpatrick in 40 minutes. In addition, both ran Sunday services throughout the year. In February 1929, the Sharvins borrowed the 13-seater Overland bus with which Margaret Anderson had been operating a somewhat ephemeral local bus service in the vicinity of Ballynahinch; later in the same year the Sharvins took over the Conway service but retained only one of the latter's buses, an 11-seater Ford. Toward the end of the 1920s the Sharvins came to an agreement with the BCDR for the issue of combined rail and road tickets to Strangford, an arrangement which continued to be honoured after the Sharvins had joined the BOC in 1933, from whom they received £1400 for their two Vulcan buses.

In September 1927 P Egner of Castlewellan began the Castlewellan Motor Service by providing a twice daily service between Castlewellan and Belfast via Clough, Downpatrick and Crossgar.[12] The section between Downpatrick and Belfast does not seem to have been worked for long, but the Castlewellan-Downpatrick service continued until the autumn of 1929 when the BOC purchased the goodwill of the route for £50, no buses changing hands in the transaction. Egner, himself, often drove his buses which were 14-seater Vulcans, but he was frequently in serious trouble with the police for over-crowding.[13]

42. Ulster & General Motor Transport Co Ltd., Karrier charabanc Reg OI 2629. The company's offices were at 59 Chichester Street, Belfast. Date, pre-1914. Courtesy HMSO. UFTM L3754/9

The distance between Downpatrick and Belfast via Crossgar is 22 miles compared with 25 miles via Killyleagh and Comber. Public transport between the two places has always used the shorter route; indeed it has never been possible to travel by public transport between the two places via Killyleagh without having to change at least once en route. Until the advent of motor transport, mail for the latter town was usually sent by rail to Comber where it was taken by horsedrawn mail cart, none of which went on beyond Killyleagh. This practice of terminating at Killyleagh continued after the motor bus of the Ulster & General Motor Transport Company took over the working of the mail just before the outbreak of the 1914–18 War.[14] Just after the war, the contract passed first to T Wallace of Killyleagh[15] who worked it with a charabanc, named *Maid of Mourne* until 1925. The contract was then taken over by S G McFarlane of Belfast who joined the BOC two years later. Other operators over the route included Robert Gilliland's Moneyreagh MS which ran a morning and evening service on weekdays between Ballygowan and Belfast, Edward Johnston of Ballynahinch (see page 27), whose Johnston Royal Mail Service provided three double workings on weekdays between Killyleagh and Comber from 1927 to 1933, Samuel Garrett and Thomas Robinson who provided a short lived joint service between Killyleagh and Belfast in 1926. After their partnership ended in 1927, Garrett began to run a bus between Belfast and Ballymacashon via Ballygowan and Florida Manor,[16] but it was short lived because T Spence, who ran the Triumph buses between Belfast and Ballynahinch, also put some of his own vehicles onto the road to Ballymacashon. In May 1930, Spence sold his Ballynahinch and Ballymacashon services to the BOC which paid him £9000 for his nine buses (1 ADC; 1 Commer; 1 Leyland; 6 Vulcan). After this the BOC, and its successors, continued to work to Ballymacashon until the mid-1960s when buses on this route ceased to work regularly east of Ballygowan. The hamlet of Derryboy, which lies half way between Saintfield and Killyleagh, has had a direct bus to Belfast since 23 March 1925 when Francis and Nathaniel McFarland of Crossgar started a service between the two places. In 1928 they sold their bus and the goodwill of the service to the BOC which, along with its successors, has continued to work it until today.

The BOC's last acquisition in the area was made in September 1932 when it paid £5000 for the four buses (2 Leyland; 2 Lancia) with which Samuel Davidson of Comber had been providing an hourly service between Comber and Belfast.[17] His buses usually covered the eight miles in half an hour whereas the trains usually took about 25 minutes (12 minutes for non-stop trains), but a single ticket on the bus cost 6d compared with 1s by rail. Davidson also ran rural services from Comber to Ballydrain and Ballyhorn and, during the summer, provided Sunday afternoon trips from Comber to Bangor. His services began in 1925 and, from the first he had to face competition from the Express MTC. However, after about a year, the latter's proprietor decided to concentrate on touring and the Express MTC withdrew from the route. Early in 1932 Davidson arranged to sell his undertakings to John McCartney of Newtownards, but the sale was vetoed by the government on the grounds that, since it operated in BOC territory, it should be offered first to the Belfast company. The BOC accepted the offer and took over Davidson's company in August 1932.

43. BOC Associated Daimler Co bus Reg XI 8749. The bus was supplied new in 1927 with a 32-seater body by Dodson to M Morrow of Bangor. This photograph was taken at Ormeau Embankment, Belfast about 1930. Photograph R Ludgate Collection UFTM L3773/10

Newry and Mourne

The BOC operated an extensive network of local services in the Newry and Mourne district as well as providing long distance workings to Belfast. Rathfriland was also the terminal for a bus route to Belfast and was the focal point for several locally owned rural services, all of which retained their independence until the NIRTB take over whereas the majority of the corresponding services at Newry had joined the BOC before 1935.

The first bus in the district arrived in 1923. It was owned by D A Crory of Rathfriland who used it to commence a daily service between Rathfriland to Belfast, via Banbridge. Between the opening and the takeover the service by the BOC in 1927, the time for the 31-mile journey to Belfast came down from 2hr 15min to 1hr 55min and the number of daily workings increased from one to three.

The bus service between Newry and Belfast began on Monday 28 July 1924.[1] It was started by R J Poots of Dromore and William Dunlop of Newry and was advertised as the Frontier Bus Service. Initially, only one double working was provided daily, the bus being timed to leave Marcus Square, Newry, at 0845 hrs and to set off on its return journey from Ormeau Avenue, Belfast, at 1800 hrs, 2hrs 20min being allowed for the 38 mile journey. By the time the company joined the BOC in 1927, it was providing six double workings and the single journey time had been reduced to two hours. Each of the Poots and Dunlop buses carried names which were prefixed by *'The Frontier'* with their smallest bus being called *'The Frontier Wasp'* as it was intended to 'sting the railway.'[12]

Five other operators working in the Newry area also joined the BOC. The first was John McCourt who had begun to run between Crossmaglen and Newry in the mid-1920s and joined the BOC in March 1928. The next was the garage owner John Nesbitt of Warrenpoint who operated a somewhat sparse service between Milltown and Newry. This began in the summer of 1928 and was sold to the BOC shortly after the death of its owner in 1930 when his only serviceable bus, a 14-seater Chevrolet, was purchased for £100. In 1932 Samuel Alexander of Markethill and Mrs Anne Sloan of Kilkeel both joined the BOC. The former had begun to operate the Renown Motor Service between Newry, Markethill and Belfast in January 1926 (see page 59). Shortly afterwards he disposed of the Markethill-Belfast section of the route to Lewis and Smith of Lambeg and, in October 1928, extended some of his Newry-Markethill workings to Armagh. His buses were given 1hr 15min to cover the 20 miles from Newry to Armagh, three double workings being usually provided. Like many other operators in inland towns throughout the province, Alexander ran buses to the seaside on Sunday afternoons during the summer, in his case they ran to Warrenpoint, patrons being charged 1s 6d single or 2s 6d return. However, his weekday time-table seems to have been over-ambitious for his resources, for he was often in trouble with the authorities because of late running and unannounced cancellations so that, in the end, his licence was withdrawn by the government in 1932. His business was acquired by the BOC, which also purchased one of Alexander's 20-seater Reo buses. Five months after this, the BOC acquired the service belonging to Mrs Anne Sloan of Kilkeel who had begun to run buses from Kilkeel to Newry in 1928, four double workings being provided; the 18 mile journey being scheduled to take an hour. For the benefit of those working on the construction of the Silent Valley Reservoir she inaugurated a twice daily service between the main construction site and Kilkeel in 1931. She also provided special workings on Sundays and Holidays of Obligation to take worshippers to church at Massfort and Kilkeel and, during the summer, ran Sunday afternoon buses from Newry to Cranfield. In 1932 Catherwood tried to purchase her business as he wanted to use her service as a feeder for his Dublin-Belfast buses which went through Newry. However, the government vetoed the transaction on the grounds that her buses ran in BOC territory and should be offered to the Belfast company first. The BOC offer was accepted and on 24 October of that year her three buses (24-seater Thornycroft, painted blue; two 32-seater Commers painted green and yellow) were sold to the Belfast company. Mrs

44. McAtees Motor Service advertisement. UFTM L2100/3

45. Market at Kilkeel, Co Down in the early 1930s with bus outside McAtee's premises. UFTM L1930/9

Sloan was an able publicist, her time-table hand-outs were headed 'SOS' followed by the slogan 'Safest Omnibus Service' and ended with the words 'Buses cleaned and disinfected after each journey.'

The last buses in the district to join the BOC belonged to David McAtee who owned a hair-dressing business in Kilkeel. In March 1924 he began to run buses, the Mourne buses between Kilkeel and Belfast via Newcastle and Ballynahinch and by 1928 he was providing five double workings to Belfast, three to Newry via Warrenpoint, and church buses on Sundays. His buses, like those belonging to his rivals, the Edgars who joined BOC in 1928, were allowed 2hr 20min for the 43 mile journey to Belfast, this was the minimum time permitted by the Government, which was ever-vigilant in seeing that the 20mph speed limit for heavy pneumatic-tyred vehicles was strictly observed. At the time the fare from Kilkeel to Belfast was 2s 6d single (4s return), whereas if one travelled by the BCDR bus from Kilkeel to Newcastle and then continued one's journey by train the cost would have been 4s single or 6s 6d return. In May 1930 McAtee accepted an offer for his service from Messrs Baird and Weir, the owners of the Imperial Bus Service, but the government forbade the sale because it considered that McAtee operated in BOC territory and so it should have the option of first refusal. Three years later he did accept an offer from the BOC and his five buses (1 Gilford; 2 Lancia; 2 Reo), which had black roofs and red bodies with white waist bands, were transferred in March 1933. The McAtee buses, like the majority of road passenger vehicles of their day, were not heated so, in winter, McAtee provided his long distance passengers with travelling rugs.

46. McAtee's bus The Mourne, *c1925. David McAtee, who owned a hairdressing business in Kilkeel, began the service on 20 March 1924. UFTM L1931/8*

47. Bus driver standing outside McAtee's premises in Kilkeel. UFTM L1932/1

Antrim, Derry, Fermanagh and Tyrone

In 1930 the NCC purchased the goodwill and other assets of all BOC services operating in the Counties of Antrim, Derry and Tyrone. The company sought to save money by substituting road bus services for its branch line (railway) passenger services which were losing money. In the transaction 12 routes worked by 59 buses changed hands for £75,500. All the routes taken over had been at one time worked by private operators, who were bought out by the BOC between 1927 and 1929. Six of these had run buses on the northern shore of Belfast Lough and the other four had provided services in the Cookstown, Magherafelt and mid-Antrim area.

The two largest Antrim companies to join the BOC were McKee's Motor Service Co Ltd and the Princess Bus Service (Smith, Weatherup and McNeilly). The former operated on the coast road between Belfast and Whitehead and the latter ran buses in Mid-Antrim and between Belfast and Cushendall via Carrickfergus, Whitehead and Larne. Both companies were started in 1924 and three years later became founder members of the BOC.

The McKee's MSC was formed in the spring of 1924 when Councillor Samuel McLoughlin MPS, James Courtney and John McKee began to run buses between Belfast and Whitehead. In July of that year their buses, which were advertised as 'Lancia Saloons' were providing ten double workings between the Albert Clock in Belfast and Whitehead, the 16-mile journey being advertised to take 1hr 15min.[1] The company, which became a private limited company on 24 November 1925[2], was well run for the councillor was a capable administrator who realised the importance of keeping his buses in good mechanical order and giving the public a thoroughly reliable transport service. James Courtney, who was a gifted mechanical engineer, looked after the fleet of 11 buses, and the intensely practical John McKee, who came from Crossgar, acted as the traffic superintendent. All three also drove buses when required, thus the early morning Sunday bus from Belfast to Whitehead was usually driven by the

48. McAtee's Gilford bus Reg JI 4293 outside his office at Kilkeel, Co Down. Courtesy B Boyle. UFTM L1528/11

councillor himself.[3] In 1926 McKees was one of the seven companies which formed the NIOC and, when the BOC was established a year later, Councillor McLoughlin, who also ran a most successful pharmacy business in Belfast, became a member of its Board. James Courtney also joined the new organisation as an engineer and, some years later, became the chief mechanical engineer of the NIRTB.

In the autumn of 1924 David Smith and Joseph McNeilly began to run a bus between Randalstown and Belfast[4] and, shortly afterwards, inaugurated bus services from Belfast to Ballymena and to Larne. In 1926 they were joined by James Weatherup of Ballyclare who had just started to run buses in East Antrim. A few years previously he had come ashore from the merchant service and had obtained a taxi. He ploughed his profits back into his business and was soon able to purchase one of the most luxurious limousines to be seen at that time in Belfast. He named it *The Princess* and, when he joined Smith and McNeilly, the three partners adopted this name for their service.

By the summer of 1926 their company had built up a fleet of 10 buses, mainly Leylands, with which they ran a service from Belfast to Ballymena via Antrim (13 double workings), Larne (10), Randalstown (4) and Cushendall[5]; there were four double workings on the last mentioned route which travelled via Carrickfergus, Whitehead and Larne and were scheduled to cover the 49 miles in 2hr 30min. Their buses worked from Library Street in Belfast and, during the summer of 1927 (their first with the BOC) many of their more up-to-date Leylands were used to provide a half-hourly service between Belfast and Portrush in an attempt to persuade

49. BOC Associated Daimler Co bus Reg. AZ 1125 at Shore Street, Cushendall, pre-1930. UFTM L1486/2

Catherwood, who also ran a half-hourly service over the same route, to join the new organisation.[6] The attempt failed and during the autumn an agreement was reached whereby Catherwood and the BOC would continue to run between Belfast and Ballymena and that all services going north of the latter would be provided by Catherwood.

After the formation of the BOC, Weatherup became one of its area managers and McNeilly resigned so that he could continue as a private operator. In 1928 McNeilly ran buses in competition with the trams in Belfast and, when a change in regulations stopped this practice, he acquired Moore's Wellington Bus Service (2 Ford; 1 Reo) of Ballymena and the Erskine Bus Service (4 Leyland) of Ballyclare. After operating these for a few months he sold both services to the NCC and then purchased two small undertakings in the Drumbo district of County Down, which he continued to work as a private operator until their compulsory acquisition by the NIRTB in 1935.

Two other operators, who at one time ran buses over the road between Randalstown and Belfast, also joined the BOC. One was James McGucken who began to run buses between Cookstown, Randalstown and Belfast in the mid-1920s and then joined the BOC in 1927, and the other was the Paragon Bus Service which became a member of the BOC in 1928. The latter was owned by Bell and Paisley and had been working between Magherafelt, Randalstown and Belfast since 1925. In the summer of 1928 it was providing three double workings over this route as well as a service between Maghera and Belfast via Bellaghy and Portglenone, a route which had been started originally by Catherwood in 1925 and transferred to the Paragon BS in April 1926. During the summer of 1927 the company entered the highly competitive coast road service between Belfast and Whitehead when it provided 19 double workings[7] by Leyland buses which had been acquired specially for this service. However, after a few months, the Paragon BS was acquired by the BOC and its former owners gave an undertaking that neither of them would be involved in running any road service which might compete with the BOC during the ensuing five years.

Elsewhere in Antrim the BOC ran services in the Braid Valley and between Crumlin and Belfast. In the mid-1920s J Alexander of Lisburn was running buses between Ballymena and Carnlough, and from Ballymena to Larne. On the former route, he had at first to compete with a one-ton Ford lorry owned by Mrs L Barr, which had been fitted with seats to carry passengers and had been in use since 1916 as the 'Mail Bus' between Ballymena, Broughshane and Carnlough. The Crumlin services had also been started in the mid-1920s when G Gale began to run the *Ballinderry Queen* via the Falls Road, and a Mr Sands put on a rival bus, named *Sanspareil*, which went through Hannahstown.

One of the oldest of the Antrim services taken over by the BOC belonged to Stewart Heddle who, in the early 1920s, had begun to carry passengers in his hackney motor car between the railway station at Ballycarry and all parts of Islandmagee. In 1925 he acquired his first motor bus and, during the next year, extended his services by working from Islandmagee to Belfast. Shortly afterwards he reorganised his schedules so that his buses could run in conjunction with those of James Crooks of Carrickfergus in providing twelve double workings between Carrickfergus and the Black Man statue in Belfast, the buses of either operator being allowed 45 minutes for their 13 mile journey. By this time Crooks had been running buses for several years and, toward the end of 1927, both he and Heddle joined the BOC.

Finally, in the autumn of 1928 the BOC purchased the two buses with which Robert Welsh had been running between Ballycarry and Belfast via Woodburn and Monkstown under the name of the Ballycarry Motor Service.

50. The Largy bus. This AEC bus ran between Enniskillen and Armagh. In the background is the residence of the master of the Model School. Photographer David Blair. UFTM L1878/3

The only BOC buses which worked regularly in Fermanagh and Tyrone were those which ran between Belfast and Enniskillen. This service began in 1926 when W Wilson of Largy, near Crumlin, began to run a bus between Armagh

Travel in Comfort

BY

The "Largy" Bus.

REGULAR DAILY SERVICE

BETWEEN

Armagh, Killylea, Caledon, Aughnacloy, Ballygawley, Augher, Clogher and Fivemiletown.

COMPETENT DRIVERS.

The "Largy" Bus ervice connects with all Trains from Belfast to Fivemiletown.

W. WILSON, Proprietor.

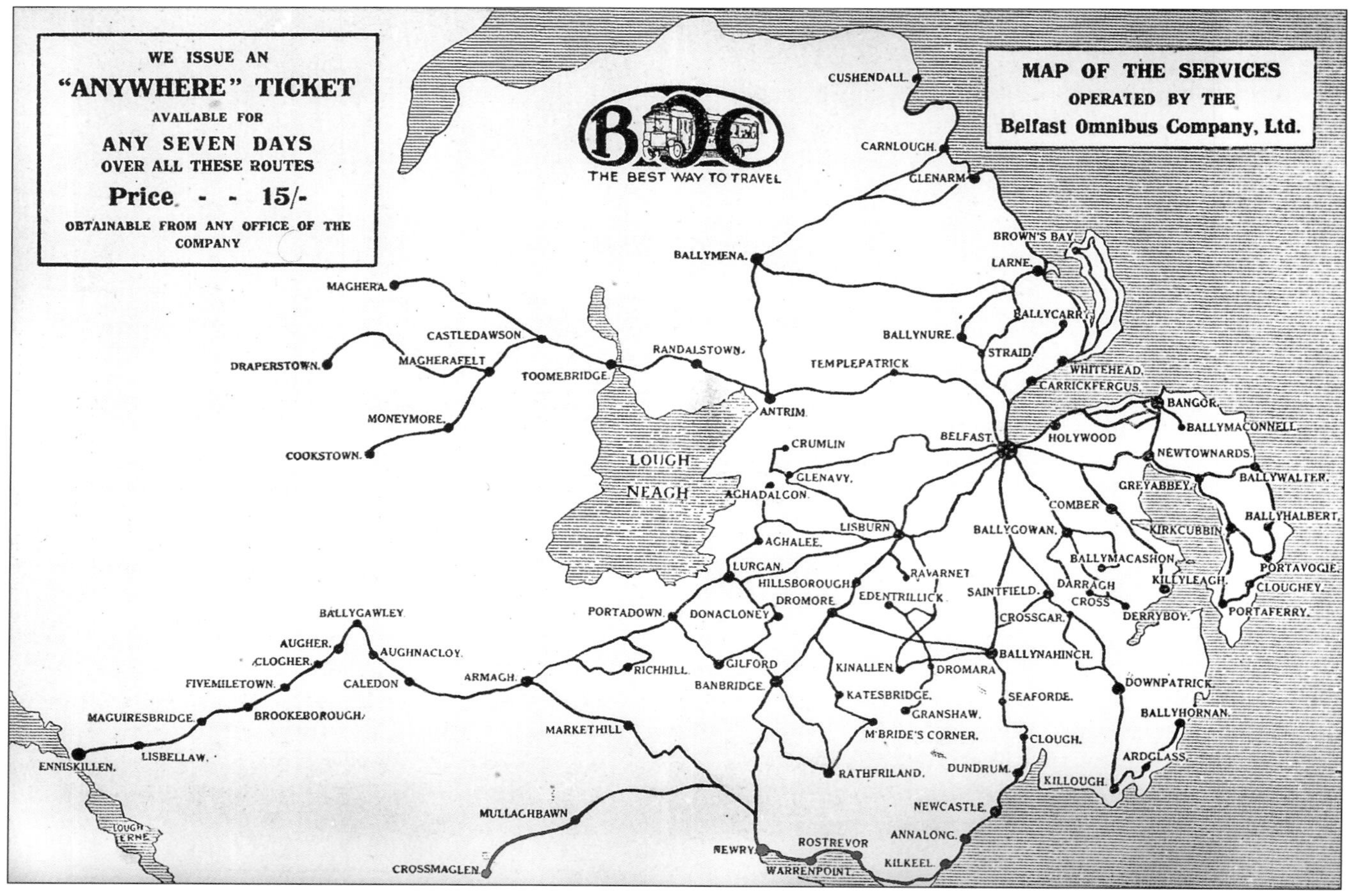

51. BOC map of services, February 1928. UFTM L3788/14

and Fivemiletown. Within a year his service had been taken over by the BOC which extended its run to Enniskillen. At first, three double workings were provided on weekdays between Belfast and Enniskillen which were scheduled to cover the 93 miles, via Armagh, in 4hr 15min. In 1996 there were ten double workings, the majority of which were routed via the M1 Motorway having been allowed 2hr 15min to get from Belfast to Enniskillen.

REFERENCES

BOC (p10–p15)

1 *Down Recorder*, 2 April 1926; *Newtownards Chronicle*, 17 April 1926.
2 *Belfast Newsletter*, 28 February 1927; 6 April 1927; PRONI Dev. 4/19.
3 *Motor Transport Year Book*, 15 (1930/31) (London), *Belfast Newsletter*, 24 April 1927.
4 Stock Exchange Year Books 1928–1935 (London).
5 *Belfast Telegraph*, 4 April 1927; PRONI UTA12/CGA/149.
6 *Investors' Chronicle*, 9 April 1927; Truth, 13 April 1927.
7 *Down Recorder*, 21 May 1927; *Newtownards Chronicle*, 30 July 1927; *Motor Transport*, 1 August 1927.
8 Brochure describing tour (Lisburn Museum).
9 PRONI COM 40/2/490/1.
10 Motor Vehicles (Traffic and Regulation) NI Act 16 & 17 Geo V, c31, 30 November 1926.

BOC North Down (p16–p23)

1 *Newtownards Chronicle*, 2 November 1967.
2 *Newtownards Chronicle*, 16 November 1907.
3 *Newtownards Chronicle*, 7 December 1907.
4 *Newtownards Chronicle*, 9 January 1908.
5 *Newtownards Chronicle*, 1 February 1908.
6 *Newtownards Almanac*, 1912, p. 179.
7 *Down Spectator*, 12 June 1914.
8 Communication, Mrs May Stevenson, Bangor.
9 *Newtownards Chronicle*, 8 January 1916.
10 PRONI COM 40/1/A31/1
11 Communication, Mrs Moss, Newtownards.
12 *Belfast Telegraph*, 11 May 1923.
13 PRONI UTA 12/CGA/154.
14 *Newtownards Chronicle*, 2 January 1926.
15 Communication, late Mr John Eadie.
16 *Newtownards Chronicle*, 23 February 1918.
17 PRONI COM 40/1/B17.
18 *Newtownards Chronicle*, 17 April 1926.
19 Stock Exchange Year Book (London) 1928.

BOC Lisburn, Lurgan and Armagh (p23–p27)

1 *Dromore Weekly Times*, 8 December 1923; 15 December 1923.
2 *Dromore Weekly Times*, 29 November 1924.
3 *Dromore Weekly Times*, 22 March 1924.
4 Communication, Councillor Mrs M L McKinney.
5 *Presbyterian Herald*, March 1945.
6 *Belfast Telegraph*, 14 June 1926; *Craigavon Times*, 16 December 1975; *Lurgan Mail*, 4 August 1947; *Lurgan Mail*, 15 September 1967.
7 PRONI COM 40/2/203.
8 PRONI COM 40/2/280.
9 *Portadown Times*, 23 June 1926.
10 *Portadown Times*, 9 June 1926.

BOC Mid-Down p27–p30

1 PRONI UTA 12/CGA/154.
2 *Belfast Telegraph*, 29 May 1964.
3 *Down Recorder*, 4 July 1925.
4 *Down Recorder*, 21 May 1927; PRONI UTA 12/CGA/154; *Newtownards Chronicle*, 30 July 1927; *Motor Transport*, 1 August 1927.
5 *Down Recorder*, 20 August 1928
6 PRONI UTA12/CGA/154.
7 Belfast Topics, June 1927.
8 *Down Recorder*, 31 March 1923.
9 *Down Recorder*, 5 November 1927.
10 *Mourne Observer*, 20 March 1920; 10 May 1979.
11 *Down Recorder*, 1 November 1919.
12 *Down Recorder*, 5 November 1927; Belfast Topics, September 1927.
13 *Down Recorder*, 7 April 1928.
14 *Newtownards Chronicle*, 10 October 1914; 8 January 1916.
15 *Belfast Telegraph*, 25 June 1921.
16 *Belfast Topics*, August 1927.
17 BCDR Director's Minutes, 7 March 1928.

BOC Newry and Mourne p31–p33

1 *Dromore Weekly Times*, 26 July 1924.
2 Communication, Mr J O'Neill, Warrenpoint

BOC Antrim, Derry, Fermanagh and Tyrone p34–p38

1 *Belfast Telegraph*, 11 July 1924.
2 PRONI COM 40/2/288.
3 Communication, Mrs W A Condy.
4 *Belfast Telegraph*, 28 October 1924.
5 *Belfast Telegraph*, 29 July 1926.
6 PRONI UTA 12/CGA/149.
7 *Belfast Telegraph*, 30 July 1927.

4. HMS Catherwood

On 7 July 1925 Harold Matthew Stuart Catherwood began to operate a bus between Maghera, Bellaghy, Portglenone, Randalstown and Antrim and, during the next three years, built up an extensive bus network between the principal towns in counties Antrim and Derry. This was at a time when official approval was unnecessary for the opening, or closing, of a service, so Catherwood was able to find out by trial and error the more lucrative routes and then develop these and discard those services on which his buses were badly patronised. In 1927 he extended his working to the Irish Free State when, in August, he opened a service between Belfast and Dublin and, in October 1930 he inaugurated a minimum fare service between Dublin and Cork. His activities in the Free State were compulsorily terminated some three years later by the Oireachtas (Dublin parliament) passing an act[1] whereby the majority of the transport undertakings in its country was transferred to its railways. In 1935, under the provision of the Northern Ireland Road and Railways Act,[2] Catherwood's organisation was merged into the Northern Ireland Road Transport Board and his fleet of 70 buses was transferred to the new undertaking on 1 October of that year.

HMS Catherwood (1899–1973) went to school in Cookstown and, at the age of sixteen, entered his father's business in Toome where, after a few years, he was put in charge of cartage. This involved the carriage of large quantities of sand which, in those days, was carried in horse-drawn carts. He was quick to see the advantage of employing motor transport and, in 1921, obtained the first tipper motor truck to be used in Ireland. All the time, however, he was nurturing an ambition to enter the road passenger transport business and in 1922 paid his first visit to Leyland Motors, and carried out a thorough investigation of the workings of the Ribble and the Crossville Motor Services in England. He was shrewd and far seeing and, during the next three years, he continued working as his father's transport manager, but was also going into 'all sorts of statistics and figures of operating costs'. Finally, he decided to buy a Leyland Edinburgh bus and, on

52. HMS Catherwood Leyland PLSC3 bus Reg XI 8902 in the late 1920s with Mr Catherwood posed beside it, probably at the Balmoral Show. Courtesy B Boyle. UFTM L3783/14

Tuesday 7 July 1925, he opened his service. Four days later he was in trouble with the police for overcrowding but, by the end of the next month, he had not only extended his original service to Belfast but had also began to run a bus between Belfast and Coleraine. During his first year he employed five buses and, after allowing for 33% depreciation, showed a profit of 300% on his capital.[3]

From the beginning Catherwood operated in a thoroughly competent manner. He concentrated on one make of vehicle, Leyland, and had a mileage contract with the India Tyre Company for the provision and maintenance of tyres, thereby ensuring that none of his buses went on the road inadequately shod. His services were operated strictly to time-table, his crews always wore uniforms and, from the beginning, a carefully monitored bell punch system was used for the issue of tickets. Maintenance was always of a high standard, indeed, in 1928 his buses ran 90,000 miles

53. HMS Catherwood Leyland bus outside Traver's Commercial Hotel, the Diamond, Donegal town. Courtesy S R Moffett. UFTM L3351/1

without incurring any serious mechanical mishap when on the road and, during the summer of that year, they carried an average of a million passengers per month. Finally, it was his company's boast that in all its ten years as an independent operator there had never been a fatal accident to a fare paying passenger.

The restrictions imposed by the government on the issue of licences for new services, which came into force late in 1928, meant that the only ways in which an operator could expand his business was by increasing the frequency of his services or by acquiring routes worked by other bus owners. Catherwood was a good business man, and realised that traffic density combined with realistic fares usually made a more worthwhile contribution to financial viability than a mere increase in route mileage. He therefore concentrated on increasing the number of fare-paying passengers on his buses by improving the quality of his service and by acquiring only those routes which could be fully integrated with services already operated by him, or would prevent a rival getting established in his territory. Thus by the time of the setting up of the BOC in 1927, he had become the largest bus owner in Ulster with about 20 modern vehicles in his fleet and was in a very sound financial position. It would, most certainly, not have been of any advantage to him to have exchanged this position for membership of a newly-formed

56. HMS Catherwood Leyland PLSC1 bus Reg XI 7372 at the Imperial Hotel, Donegall Place, Belfast, 1926. UFTM L3237/7

57. Hutchinson's Reo bus (possibly Reg IW 3289) seen here outside the premises of John Hill, the Reo agent, Seymour Street, Belfast, 1928. UFTM L1527/12

Hutchinsons continued to run a bus between Limavady, Myroe and Dungiven until the NCC bought this service from them in October 1929. R J Pattison Nutt owned a bicycle shop in Limavady and started 'Nutt's Saloon Motor Service' between Limavady and Derry shortly after Hutchinson Bros went on the road and, by 1926, he was providing five double workings between Limavady and Derry. He also ran a bus between Derry and Dungiven, a route which had been pioneered by D R Roberts of Derry in 1913. Competition between Catherwood and Nutt became very intense in the months after Hutchinson had been taken over; this and a fire which destroyed several of Nutt's buses in November 1928, ultimately forced him to sell out and, on 10 April 1929, his three buses (one 24-seater Lancia; two 35-seater Leyland) were acquired by Catherwood. After this Catherwood provided a minimum of 11 double workings between Derry and Portrush during the summer, the majority of which connected with his Belfast-Portrush service at Coleraine.

During the winter of 1927/28 the North Star Motor Service between Belfast, Ballymoney and Ballycastle was taken over. This company was owned by Moore of Wellington Street, Ballymena, and had usually provided three double workings to and from Ballycastle, and this frequency was maintained by Catherwood. The service of three other operators were taken over between 1929 and 1930. On 1 January 1929 Catherwood acquired the Ballymena-Garvagh service of the Bann Motor Service Co Ltd. This organisation[5] had been incorporated on 1 March 1927 and had run buses between Coleraine and Magherafelt, and from Ballymena to Garvagh. The latter had been worked by a 24-seater Lancia which was acquired by Catherwood for £500 at the take over. Its new owner recast its timetable so that its arrivals and departures at Ballymena connected with his Belfast-Portrush service. Six months later Catherwood acquired the operating licences held by James D White and David Weir who both lived in Bushmills and had been operating rival bus services between Bushmills and Coleraine from the mid-1920s. At the take over, the former held the mail contract and owned two buses which provided four double workings, whereas the latter had only one bus which ran twice daily over a different route to Coleraine. Both charged the same fare (1s single, 1s 6d return) for the 8–10 mile journey. A few weeks after their acquisition, Catherwood extended some of the Coleraine-Bushmills workings to Portballintrae, permission for which had previously been given to Weir in the spring of 1930.

Catherwood's principal services were between Belfast, Portrush and Derry and the important trans-border route between Belfast and Dublin. The Belfast-Portrush route was given the service number '1' and the Coleraine-Derry service became '2' when route numbers were introduced in August 1929. On Service No 1 half-hourly workings were provided during the summer and 16 round trips during the rest of the year, heated buses being used on the latter from 1929 onwards. An additional all year service was also run to Portrush which used the main road between Belfast and Ballymoney and then proceeded via Bushmills; three double workings were usually provided, the time allowed in 1929 being 3hr 15min, which was just a quarter of an hour longer than by the direct route. During the summer a bus ran once a day from Belfast to Portrush along the coast via Carrickfergus, Larne, Cushendall and Ballycastle, and three double workings were provided which followed the main road from Belfast to Ballymena and then turned north-east via Glenariff to Cushendall, after which they went through Ballycastle to Portrush. Buses on the latter run were not permitted to pick up or set down local passengers between Ballymena and Cushendall; this was a government ruling designed to protect the interests of local bus operators who had to maintain all year round services, which were kept just financially viable by the summer trade between Ballymena and the coast. In addition to the services just mentioned Catherwood also ran buses between Gortin (Co Tyrone) and Derry, two limited stop services between Belfast, Ballymena, Kilrea, Limavady and Derry and, in May 1929, came to an agreement with the corporation of the city of Londonderry to provide municipal transport services within the city. A year previous to this he had gained considerable experience in the operation of municipal services when 38 of his buses had taken part in the Belfast Bus War.

On 22 August 1927 Catherwood opened a service between Belfast and Dublin, four round trips being worked each weekday by Leyland (PLSC3) buses with 17-seater bodies built specially for the service by Hall Lewis. At first 4½ hours were needed for the 102-mile journey between Upper Library Street in Belfast and Eden Quay in Dublin and all buses made a five minute stop in Dundalk. Within a few months a rival service was started by S H Weir and A S Baird of Belfast who traded as the International Bus Service. By the summer of 1929 the two companies were together providing a minimum of nine double workings between the two cities, the fares being 10s single and 15s return whereas the railway charged 14s single and 26s 6d return. On the other hand, the use of these buses for short journeys was discouraged by charging slightly higher fares than those by normal bus, thus a return ticket from Belfast to Newry cost 6s 8d if travelling by Catherwood's Dublin service, compared with 6s 1d by any of the other operators such as the BOC. In October 1929 the five Gilford buses (mainly 24-seaters) used by the International BS were purchased by Catherwood for £8000. On the demise of the International BS, which had always run on every day of the week, there was no Sunday service, but after a few weeks the GNR was authorised to provide two double workings on Sundays between the two capitals. Catherwood also introduced feeder services to boost his Belfast-Dublin route. The first of these began late in 1927 when the feeder buses left Belfast about an hour before the departure of some of the direct Dublin buses. The former travelled through Portadown, Armagh and Markethill to Newry where they connected with the main Belfast-Dublin service. There were few customers and the service was withdrawn after a few weeks. Indeed, Catherwood never had much success in County Armagh, for a service between Belfast and Derry via Portadown, Armagh, Ballygawley and Omagh, which he started in December 1927, also lasted for only a few weeks.[6] Until the opening of the Dublin-Cork service in 1930, this was the longest route operated by Catherwood with the 110-mile journey being scheduled to take 5hr 35min. The goodwill of the northern part of this Derry service passed to C H Donaghy of Omagh and, throughout 1928, the schedules for Donaghy's Omagh-Derry buses were published in Catherwood's timetables. In 1932 Catherwood made another attempt to run a feeder service to Newry. In September of that year he arranged to purchase the buses which Mrs Anne Sloan ran between Kilkeel and Newry, but the take over was not sanctioned by the Government as it was considered that Mrs Sloan operated in BOC territory.

Catherwood's next venture in the Free State was the takeover of the Irish Omnibus Company's Derry-Sligo service on 13 August 1928. This route crossed the border between Derry and St Johnston and then went through Raphoe, Stranorlar, Donegal, Ballyshannon and Bundoran, the 85-mile journey taking about 4hr 15min. About a year later a feeder service was started in which buses left Derry a short time before the departure of the Sligo buses and travelled via St Johnston, Lifford and Castlefinn to connect with the through buses at Stranorlar. In

May of the same year another feeder service was started between Portnoo, Glenties, Ardara, Killybegs and Donegal, passengers being able to join the Derry-Sligo buses at the last mentioned place. On the other hand, the Northern Ireland government never allowed him to operate between Enniskillen and Derry since it maintained there was already an adequate bus service on this route.

Two other Catherwood developments also took place in the Free State in 1929. In December 1929 he started to run a bus between Clones, Newbliss, Ballybay, Castleblayney, Carrickmacross and Dundalk, the timetable being so arranged that passengers connected with the Belfast-Dublin service at the latter place; also, in the same month he began a suburban service which ran between central Dublin and The Bailey on the Hill of Howth. Both were closed down after a few weeks but the Clones service was replaced by one running between Carrickmacross, Ardee, Collon and Drogheda, where a connection was made with the Dublin-Belfast buses. A few months later, this working was cut back at Ardee and, at about the same time, a new service was started between Clogher (Co Louth) and Drogheda. At least four double workings were provided on each of the two services, which were well supported and continued until the company's withdrawal from the south in 1933. The last service to be established in the Free State was the limited stop, minimum fare, service between Dublin and Cork which began on Thursday 7 October 1930. Two double workings were provided, the buses passing through Naas, Kildare, Portlaoise, Abbeyleix, Cashel, Cahir, Mitchelstown and Fermoy with the morning bus from Cork and the evening one from Dublin connecting with buses to and from Belfast; through tickets between Belfast and Cork being issued at 26s 6d single and 47s return, compared with 34s 9d and 61s 10d by rail. The Dublin-Cork service was designated in the timetables as Service No 22, the highest route number to be used by Catherwood. The operating of Service 22 passed to the Irish Omnibus Company when Catherwood's buses were prevented from running in the Free State.

A year before Catherwood opened his Dublin-Cork service, a sleeper bus ran for a few weeks between the two cities.[7] It was owned by the Irish Sleeper Omnibus Service which was managed by the Dublin tour operator T J Furey. The interior of the bus was somewhat similar to that of a standard North American sleeping car, with its passengers occupying longitudinal berths on either side of a central gangway from which they were separated by curtains. The body of the coach which was built by Strachans of London, was mounted on an AEC Model 426 chassis and could accommodate 32 passengers on bench type seats which could be converted into eight berths for night use. The bus was scheduled to leave Cork at 2200 hrs and, after calling at Limerick at 0100 hrs, was due in Dublin in time for its passengers to catch the morning mail boat sailing from Dun Laoghaire. A similar schedule was advertised for the return to Cork. The first public appearance of the bus after its arrival in Ireland was on a demonstration run from Dublin to Belfast on 29 December 1928.

In 1921 the Londonderry Corporation replaced its trams by a bus service, which enjoyed a local transport monopoly within its city until the municipal Bus War spread from Belfast to Derry in 1928. Catherwood, who had been heavily involved in the Belfast fracas, moved to Derry in

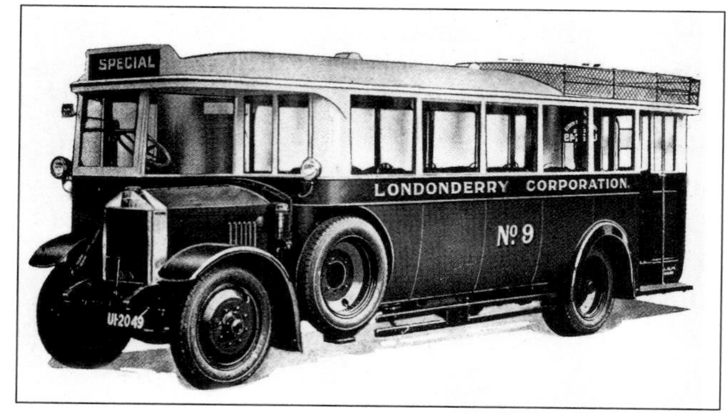

58. Londonderry Corporation Albion PMA 28 bus Reg UI 2049. This was one of five Albions purchased new by the corporation in 1928. They were sold to HMS Catherwood in May 1929. UFTM L3745/6

54. HMS Catherwood conductor and driver, c1931. The conductor's name was Moffett who went on to become a driver sometime in 1932. He continued to drive buses for the NIRTB until 1945 when he went to work as a driver for Inglis & Co bakers, Belfast. Courtesy S R Moffett. UFTM L3315/5

55. Driver Moffett with HMS Catherwood bus in Donegal town where he met his future wife. Date, c 1933. Courtesy S R Moffett. UFTM L3315/6

coalition of small proprietors, many of whom lacked the managerial skill and business ability needed to control a large undertaking. The BOC was particularly anxious that he should join it and, when persuasion failed, inaugurated a half-hourly service to compete with him on the road between Belfast and Portrush. Not only did he fight off this challenge, but a few months later, was able to persuade the BOC to limit its activities to the part of this road which lay between Belfast and Ballymena, thereby allowing him to regain his monopoly of the Belfast-Portrush traffic. From 1929 onwards he had to meet very severe competition from the NCC which, with the financial resources of the LMS behind it, began to take over all the bus operators in Antrim, Derry and East Tyrone which were still outside the Catherwood network.

Like 1925, 1926 was also a year of expansion, despite the transfer in April of his initial service (Maghera-Belfast via Randalstown) to the Paragon Bus Service of Belfast. This was the only route which Catherwood ever sold voluntarily during his ten years as an omnibus proprietor. By mid-summer he was providing an hourly service between Belfast and Portrush, with buses leaving the city on the half hour and Portrush at five minutes past the hour, 3hr 55min being allowed for the 62-mile journey. His passengers were charged 5s single, 8s return, with weekend returns being available at 7s. In addition his buses were running between Coleraine and Derry, via Limavady over a route in which Hutchinson Bros and R J Pattison Nutt were already well established.[4] Hutchinson Bros owned a garage in Limavady, and on 18 March 1922 had begun to run a bus between their home town and Derry, five years later they owned several 20-seater Reos which were providing 12 double workings over this route, four of the runs being extended to Coleraine and Portrush. Catherwood took over their Derry-Portrush service in 1928 but the

59. HMS Catherwood bus at the Guildhall, Ship Quay Place, Londonderry. (From a postcard). UFTM L3701/3

September and by May 1929 had not only attained a dominant position on the roads in the area, but had also persuaded the corporation to sell him five of its Albion buses and to give him a concession for the provision of public transport in its city. In return, its citizens were given a good service (ten minute intervals on some routes) at fares ranging from 1d to 3d, a special attraction being weekly tickets giving unlimited travel on all three of the city's bus routes for 3s. In 1932 Catherwood opened a central bus station in Foyle Street, but in Belfast his buses always worked from the kerb side adjacent to his garage and head offices in Upper Library Street.

In 1933 the Dublin parliament passed an act transferring the working of the greater part of the passenger and freight road services to the railways. As a result of this Catherwood's transport interests in the Free State (Dublin-Cork service excepted) were acquired by the GNR, and his 24 Leyland buses working south of the border became railway property. Through workings on the Belfast-Dublin service then ceased, but passengers could still travel by road between the two capitals provided they changed buses at Newry and, if necessary, at Dundalk. At the same time, the through Derry-Sligo service was taken over by the GNR and today the route is still open being worked by Bus Éireann, a subsidiary of CIE, the buses of which are now scheduled to cover the whole route (85 miles) in 2hr 45min.

Catherwood was the first omnibus operator in Ireland to provide 'All-in' tours covering all parts of the island. These began in 1929 and for about £13 patrons enjoyed a week's touring by coach, with accommodation in good hotels and the services of a guide-courier; shortly afterwards similar tours were run to Scotland. The company also issued 'Anywhere' tickets at 30s which permitted their holders to travel where and when they liked over the Catherwood network for a week. During the summer, day tours were run from the principal centres and Mystery Tours were also provided; the latter gave their patrons a worthwhile drive and at least an hour in a seaside resort. The Mystery Tours from Belfast usually left Upper Library Street on Wednesdays and Saturdays at 1430 hrs and arrived back about seven hours later. Portrush was the usual venue for the Belfast tours and, for an inclusive fare of 2s 6d, patrons had several hours at the seaside and a free tea in the Trocadero Restaurant (owned by Catherwood); the tours were very popular and quite often five or more double deckers would be required to cope with all who turned up.

Catherwood's first bus was a 32-seater Leyland which he purchased in the early summer of 1925. It was followed by a low-slung Fageol safety coach built by Warwick Wright Ltd and fitted with a Hall Scott engine. It was painted in a shade of light

60. Accident involving HMS Catherwood bus in the Coleraine area. This vehicle is a 32-seater Leyland. Courtesy B Boyle. UFTM L3782/11

blue which pleased Catherwood so much that he adopted it as his fleet livery, indeed Leylands used to refer to the colour as 'Catherwood blue'. The Fageol's dimensions (29ft × 8ft) were above the legal maxima (27ft × 7ft 6in) permitted at that time but this seems to have been overlooked by the authorities. The bus was very safe and its great stability was well demonstrated when it remained upright after going through a hedge when avoiding a collision.

In 1926 Leylands brought out the first of its PLSC3 chassis which had been specifically designed to take bus bodies. Previous to this, the majority of manufacturers had used the same design of chassis for both lorries and buses. The new design enabled body builders to reduce floor height above the ground by about a foot thereby making their vehicles more easily accessible for passengers as well as increasing their safety by reducing the height of their centre of gravity. The PLSC3 chassis had a wheel base of 16ft 5in and could take a body 26ft long. It was powered by a 5.1 litre petrol engine and, when fitted with a Leyland body, had an unladen weight of about 4½ tons. The majority of the Catherwood buses acquired in 1927 and 1928 were of this type which were referred to in the trade as Leyland Lions. Between 1929 and 1934 the company acquired 18 of the larger Leyland Tigers (TS 2–6) which had a wheel base of 17ft 6in and were powered by a 6.8 litre petrol engine. In 1931 the first of the Leyland Titan (TD1) double-deckers were obtained by the company. These had 52-seater low-bridge bodies giving them a total height of 13ft 6in which was attained by having a sunken

61. HMS Catherwood Leyland PLSC 3 bus Reg XI 8902 with a 29-seater body by Hall Lewis, seen here on a tour of the North-west. Courtesy B Boyle. UFTM L3783/16

62. HMS Catherwood Leyland Tiger TS1 bus Reg AZ 3030 on tour in Co Donegal. The driver is John McMaster who later became a depot manager. Courtesy B Boyle. UFTM L3784/2

gangway on one side of the upper deck from which access was gained to transverse bench seats accommodating either three or four passengers. All double-decker buses working between Belfast and Antrim had to make compulsory stops at Templepatrick and Dunsilly and then proceed slowly under the centres of the railway arches at these places, otherwise their roofs would have collided with the masonry of the bridges.

The buses used on the Belfast-Dublin service seated only 17 passengers and have been very adequately described in the transport journals of their day, such as in *Motor Transport* of 1 December 1927. They had Leyland Lion PLSC3 chassis for which special bodies had been built at

63. HMS Catherwood Leyland Royal Tiger TS2 bus Reg AZ 4528 outside their works in Donegall Road, Belfast. The roof mounted luggage compartment was accessible from the saloon interior. Date, 1930. R Ludgate Collection. UFTM L3773/6

64. *HMS Catherwood Leyland bus Reg XI 6037 with the Leyland motor's demonstrator 'Lowbridge' bus at the railway bridge Templepatrick, Co Antrim in the late 1920s. Courtesy B Boyle. UFTM L3784/6*

65. *HMS Catherwood Leyland TD2 double decker bus. The vehicle is brand new and does not yet have its registration plates. Courtesy B Boyle. UFTM L3784/5*

Hall Lewis. Luggage was carried in lockers beneath the floor, and passengers were seated two on one side and one on the other of a central gangway, and each seat was provided with a folding table. In addition there was a chemical toilet and a small buffet on each bus, catering being provided by the Carlton restaurant in Belfast. Each of the first four buses to go into service had different interior finishes: walnut, rosewood, french walnut and mahogany. Like all the other buses in the company's fleet they were painted Catherwood blue and lined in white with the name HMS Catherwood in roman capitals below the windows and below this the company's monogram which was surrounded by a garter. Mudguards were usually painted black and

66. HMS Catherwood Leyland TD2 double-decker bus. Courtesy B Boyle. UFTM L3784/7

wheels were white. However, the Dublin-Belfast buses did not carry letter-boxes for post as did many of those working between Belfast and Portrush and from Belfast to Ballycastle.

During his first three years Catherwood ran his business as a partnership but, as it grew larger, it became expedient that it should become a limited company. On 20 July 1928 HMS Catherwood Ltd was incorporated as a private company[8] with a nominal capital of £25,000; the majority of the shares were held by the Catherwood family with a few being distributed to those closely associated with them such as W A Agnew, who was their manager, and the Northern Bank. In 1932 the controlling interest in the firm was sold to the London-based transport holding company, Thomas Tilling, and the Catherwood capital structure was reorganised to give Tillings a 58% stake with the rest of the capital in the hands of the Catherwood family. The company had now become a subsidiary of the Tilling Group which nominated two directors to its board. These were H C Merrett, who had played an important role in the formation of the BOC in the mid-1920s, and S Kennedy of Shortlands, Kent; at the same time HMS Catherwood was given a seat on the Tilling main board. However, within the next three years, HMS Catherwood Ltd had lost its bus fleet, for the passing of the Northern Ireland Road and Railway Transport Act of 1935 transferred his road passenger business to the NIRTB. It included 70 buses, 66 of which were Leylands. The Catherwood shareholders received 59,000 A and 41,000 B stocks in the new organisation. HMS Catherwood Ltd went into voluntary liquidation, with N W Rolfe from the United Bus Company, Northampton, as liquadator on 27 February 1936. The company was finally wound up on 10 July 1939, just 14 years and three days after HMS Catherwood had run his first bus.

HMS Catherwood was the only one of the early omnibus proprietors in Ulster to become a large scale operator and to retain control of his organisation from its inception until its compulsory acquisition by the NIRTB. When the latter occurred he was still in his mid-thirties and had become one of the most prominent men in the Ulster of his day. He did not, however, confine all his attention to road interests for, in 1928, he was involved in trying to start a flying-boat service between Belfast and Liverpool and ten years later he became interested in reviving the summer steamship service between Portrush and Ardrossan. In many ways he resembled Charles Bianconi (1786–1875), who was the first road transport operator in Ireland to realise the commercial importance of absolute dependability brought about by good routine maintenance, a well-paid and contented staff, and competent supervision. Furthermore, neither C Bianconi nor HMS Catherwood made a practice of working on Sundays.

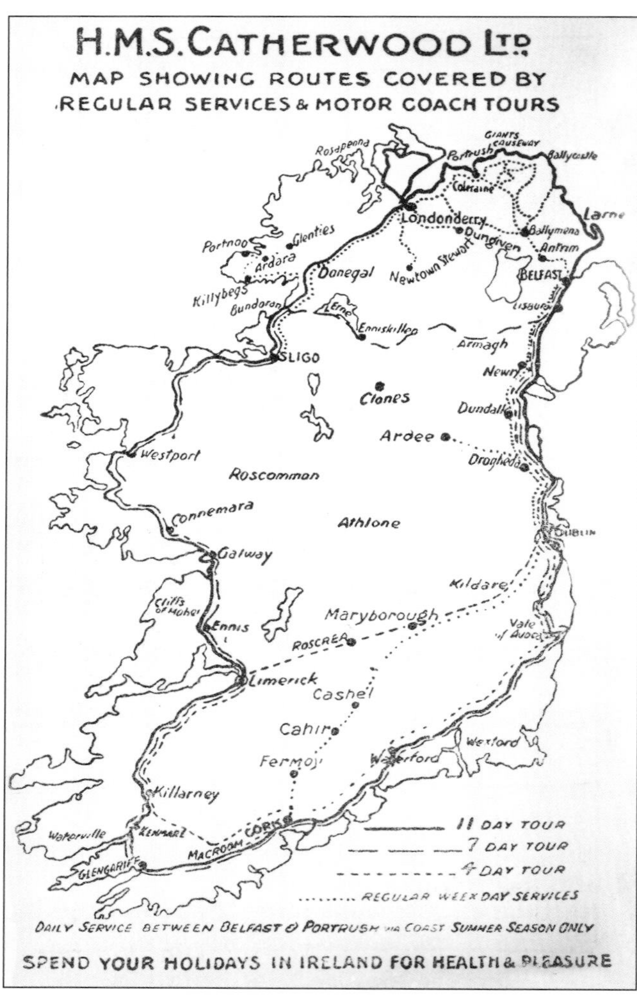

67. HMS Catherwood route map. UFTM L3894/8

REFERENCES

1 Road Traffic Act, No 11, 29 June 1933
2 Road and Rail Transport (NI) Act, 25&26 Geo V, c15 16 July 1935
3 Communication, HMS Catherwood (August 1957)
4 *Londonderry Sentinel*, 6 February 1980
5 PRONI Com 40/2/390
6 *Armagh Guardian* 16 December 1927
7 *Modern Transport* 5 January 1929
8 PRONI Com 40/2/490/1

General:
Belfast Topics July/December 1927
HMS Catherwood, Timetables

5. Great Northern Railway (Ireland)

68. Mourne Mountain Touring Company solid-tyred Dennis bus Reg IJ 719 at the GNR Hotel, Warrenpoint. Lawrence Collection. UFTM L1931/10

The buses of the Great Northern Railway (Ireland) operated mainly in those parts of the country which could be regarded as GNR territory. This included part of Armagh with its busy road between Portadown and Belfast as well as the comparatively thinly populated counties in the north-west of the Province. The railway began to buy up private bus operators in 1929, but four years elapsed before it had become the principal road service operator throughout its territory and, even then, it had failed to take over any of the private operators domiciled in either Donegal or Fermanagh.

The GNR began to operate its own passenger road services on 28 January 1929, when it started to run local services in Drogheda and, in the following month, it acquired the Louth and Meath Omnibus Company, whose buses plied between Dublin and Drogheda. On 30 March of the same year it spread its activities to Northern Ireland by purchasing the business of J & R Irwin of Lurgan and, during the next three years, it acquired the assets of eighteen other operators who ran buses elsewhere in the province of Ulster.

Newry and Mourne

The earliest motor buses to operate in GNR territory were stationed at Warrenpoint where, in June 1913, G B Morgan, the licensee of the Great Northern Hotel, acquired three 13-seater

69. Mourne Mountain Touring Company Dennis charabanc at Warrenpoint, 1913. UFTM L2098/7

Dennis charabancs for his Mourne Mountain Touring Company.[1] They were used mainly for running day tours in the Mourne Mountains until war time restrictions forced them to be withdrawn. Shortly after this, on 23 May 1916, Norton & Co of Kilkeel began to run a 16-seater Selden motor bus for passengers and mail between Kilkeel and the railway station in Warrenpoint.[2] At the time the Nortons had been running a posting establishment in Kilkeel for over 40 years, their parent company Norton & Shaw of London having been invited to come to Ireland by the Earl of Kilmorey shortly after the opening of the steamer service between Greenore and Holyhead[3] in 1873. By the end of the 1870s the company had become established in South Down where it owned the Woodside and Mourne (re-named Great Northern) Hotels at Rostrevor; ran horse-drawn long cars between Warrenpoint and Newcastle, Downpatrick and

70. Solid-tyred charabanc Reg V 646 at the Mourne Hotel, Rostrevor, Co Down. (From a Lawrence postcard). UFTM L3701/4

Strangford, and from Newtownards to Portaferry; operated ferries at Greencastle and Warrenpoint; and had a controlling interest in the horse-drawn tramway which ran between Warrenpoint and the quay at Rostrevor. In the early 1880s it sold its County Down road services to its local manager, H A Matier, who had been at one time an employee of the Belfast and Northern Counties Railway.[4] Matier continued to trade under the name of Norton and Company until his undertaking was acquired by the GNR on 6 February 1930 when his two 14-seater Fords were purchased by the railway.

Two months after the arrival of the Selden bus at Kilkeel, the Belfast and County Down Railway took delivery of a Dennis bus which immediately began to run between Kilkeel and the company's station at Newcastle.[5] The 1914–18 War was then entering its third year, and the two operators had great difficulty in getting adequate fuel supplies for their buses. In September 1916 the Nortons reverted to working all their services between Kilkeel and Warrenpoint by horse-drawn long cars and sold their Selden to the BCDR. At the end of the war Norton & Co acquired another motor bus and then gradually improved its services until, by the late 1920s, it was providing seven double workings between Warrenpoint and Kilkeel in which the 12 mile journey took 40 minutes. When requested by the Post Office two of these workings would often be extended to Annalong.

The other owner operating buses in the Newry area was Peter Maguire of Omeath who owned the Omeath Motor Service. In the summer of 1928 he was providing four double workings between Carlingford and Newry. In July of the following year, the Keenan brothers of Carlingford began to run a bus between

71. Fawcett's tour buses at GNR Great Victoria Street Station, Belfast, 25 July 1934 at 10.03am. These buses were used in a combined road and rail tour to Dublin. Photographer A R Hogg. Courtesy B Boyle. UFTM L3779/13

72. Twelve Fawcett's tour buses, 27 July 1934. These Albion vehicles were registered to the GNR. Photographer A R Hogg. Courtesy B Boyle. UFTM L3779/12

73. Fawcett tours Albion PT 65 bus Reg AZ 9551 at Portrush Hotel, Portrush, 26 July 1934. Fawcett's owned the Antrim Arms Hotel in Antrim town. Photographer A R Hogg. R Ludgate Collection. UFTM L3773/9

Dundalk and Newry which went via Carlingford and Omeath but, as Maguire was already licenced to run buses into Newry, the Keenans were not permitted by the Northern Ireland government to take up or set down passengers on the four miles of road between the border and Newry. Within three months the Keenans reduced their service from daily to bi-weekly (Tuesday and Thursday) and, by the end of the year had closed down their service. In May 1931 Maguire extended his services to Dundalk and on 15 November of the following year he sold his business to the GNR for £2500, a price which may have included a large element for goodwill as the catalogue price of his two 20/24-seater Guys was of the order of £1900.

County Antrim

The railway acquired only one service which ran entirely within County Antrim. This worked from the Diamond, near Crumlin, to Belfast via Crumlin and Dundrod and had been started in 1923 by W Dow who then lived in Crumlin. He used a 20-seater Gilford which he named the *Diamond Bus* and, until his acquisition by the GNR in January 1930, his bus was timed to cover the 17 miles between Crumlin and Belfast in an hour.

County Armagh

In addition to the acquisition of services in County Antrim and County Down, the GNR took over the services run by eight proprietors in County Armagh, of whom four worked in the Lurgan area, two in the vicinity of Portadown and two served Keady. Its first acquisition was that owned by the Lurgan shopkeepers James and Robert Irwin. The Irwins planned to operate bus services between Belfast and the principal towns in west Down. During the winter of 1925/26, they

74. GNR Leyland LT 2 buses outside Coltness Coachworks which were built new in 1931. One of the vehicles is registered AZ 7642. Courtesy B Boyle. UFTM L3780/1

75. GNR Albion PT 65 bus Reg AZ 9556 at College Square, Belfast. Front seat passenger is Mr Shanahan, a bus inspector who always wore a flower in his buttonhole. Courtesy B Boyle. UFTM L1529/2

began to run buses between Lurgan and Belfast, between Banbridge, Newry and Warrenpoint, as well as between Rathfriland and Newry. A year later they decided to concentrate on the Lurgan-Belfast route and withdrew their other two services. Early in 1927 they obtained two Maudslay safety coaches which were among the earliest of this type of vehicle in Ireland, the first being the low-slung Fageol which Catherwood had purchased in the previous year. By the end of 1927 the Irwins were providing six double workings between the kerb sides in Market Street, Lurgan, and Queen Street in Belfast. Shortly afterwards they obtained seven Dennis buses (one 31-seater; six 20-seater) which enabled them to commence a half- hourly service to the city. This frequency was maintained by the GNR when it took over the Irwins' business on 28 March 1929, a purchase which enabled the railway to commence running its first bus service north of the border. However, the GNR buses continued to work to the kerb side in Queen Street, Belfast until 1931, when all its buses serving Belfast were diverted to the NCC Bus Station in Smithfield.

Six months after the railway had got possession of the Irwin buses it took over James Winter's Eclipse Motor Transport Company.[6] This had been formed in the summer of 1927 when Winter acquired the Blytheswood Auto Service and changed its name to the Eclipse MT Co. At that time the Blytheswood company was about a year old and its principal interest was in running day tours from Belfast;[7] but in its early days it had also run a 14-seater bus for a few weeks between Armagh and Fivemiletown and even in this short period, had got into serious trouble with the authorities for overcrowding.[8] At about the time of the formation of the Eclipse MT Co, Winter began a service to Dungannon on which his buses started from the Eclipse Café in College Square East in Belfast. Shortly afterwards he got possession of two Reo 20-seaters *(Moy Queen; Omagh Queen)* which a Tyrone operator, named McDowell, had been running between Omagh and Dungannon from the beginning of 1927. This acquisition enabled Winter to extend his service to Omagh and, by the end of the year, the Eclipse buses were providing three double workings between Belfast and Omagh via Lurgan, Portadown, Dungannon and Ballygawley as well as two double workings between Dungannon and Omagh via Pomeroy. Buses on the first route were scheduled to cover the 66 miles between Belfast and Omagh in 4hr 15min. Winter sold his six buses (4 Dennis; 1 Graham-Dodge; 1 Lancia) to the railway on 16 September 1929. After the takeover, the new owners continued to provide a similar service and increased the coverage between Dungannon and Portadown by running some buses via The Moy, and Ardress and others via Tamnamore. In the meantime, Winter was appointed as GNR road service manager in Dungannon, but he seems to have had difficulty by adapting himself to his new position. He was a man who liked to be his own master and, shortly after taking up his appointment, arranged for the railway to take over the Regent Bus Service of Coalisland, but failed to keep his employers fully informed of his action, hence the purchase was never ratified, and he left GNR employment. By May 1931 he had completed most of the formalities for the setting up of the County Donegal Motor Service which was to have been an amalgamation of four Donegal bus operators, all of whom worked into the city of Derry. However, the Northern Ireland government was so tardy in issuing the necessary licences for the running of the buses between the border and the city that the venture had to be abandoned, after which Winter retired from the bus world and became a successful property developer in Belfast. Nevertheless, despite the setback over the issue of licences, all the buses involved in the CDMS were taken over by the Londonderry & Lough Swilly Railway toward the end of the year, when their new owner seems to have had little difficulty in getting the necessary licences for working over the four miles of road between the city and the border.

On 8 March 1930 the railway took over the Renown MS from Lewis & Smith of Lambeg. This partnership owned two blue buses (14-seater Overland; 20-seater Dennis) which provided two

76. GNR Albion PT 65 bus Reg AZ 9546. This vehicle was supplied new in 1932, fitted with a Weymann 30-seater body. Courtesy B Boyle. UFTM L3780/6

round workings between Belfast, Lurgan, Tandragee and Markethill, being scheduled to cover the 34 miles in 2hr 15min. The running of through buses between Belfast and Markethill by this circuitous route was continued by the GNR, and its successors, for over 40 years but today those wanting to travel over it from Belfast to Markethill have to change buses at Lurgan. The service began originally on 30 January 1926 when Samuel Alexander of Markethill began to operate his Renown buses between Newry and Belfast via Markethill, Tandragee and Lurgan.[9] (See page 32.) About a year later he sold the Markethill-Belfast section to Lewis & Smith who continued to use the name Renown, and Alexander, himself, also used the same name for the truncated service, which he continued to work between Newry and Markethill until he sold his 20-seater Reo to the BOC in 1932.

The Repulse Bus Service was the railway's last acquisition in the Lurgan district. It was started in the summer of 1927 by J McAlinden of Lurgan, running a Sunday bus to convey worshippers from Gawleys Gate to Lurgan. A year later, he and P McSherry, trading as the Repulse Bus Service, began to run buses on weekdays between Lurgan and Aghalee via Whitehall, four double workings being provided on which the single journey took about 20 minutes. On 6 May 1930 they disposed of their service and their two 20-seater Guys to the GNR and, by the end of the year, the railway had integrated the former Repulse Service with its own Aghalee-Belfast workings, thereby providing an additional route between Lurgan and Belfast. Three decades later, on 6 May 1966, these workings were taken over by Sureline Coaches Ltd of Lurgan. This was a privately-owned company, the buses of which provided a network of services in the Lurgan area as well as workings to Banbridge, Portadown and the new estates in Craigavon. However, between 1984 and 1988 it closed down during which its services gradually reverted to Ulsterbus, but during its short period of activity it was one of the first omnibus operators in the British Isles to abandon weekly and monthly season tickets in favour of multiple journey tickets.

The railway took over the services provided by two operators in the Portadown district. One was James Grew who, on 27 May 1931, was paid £145 for the 14-seater Morris with which he had been working a shuttle service between the town centre and the railway station at Portadown. The service had begun in the late 1920s and survived until just before the station was moved from the east to the west bank of the Bann on 5 October 1970, by which time it was being worked as Ulsterbus Service No 68. The other Portadown take-over occurred on 23 December 1929 when the railway acquired the eight buses (1 AEC; 1 Dennis; 1 Lancia; 5 Reo) of the United Bus Company of Tandragee. Within a year the GNR disposed of four of the 20-seater Reos to the County Donegal Railways who used them for a few years running between Killybegs, Ardara and Glenties, after which two were broken up and two rebuilt as railcar trailers. The United MS was formed in the mid-1920s and in July 1929 took over the three buses (1 AEC; 1 Dennis; 1 Reo) with which James Bleakney of Ballyreagh, Portadown, had been operating his Imperial Bus Service between Tandragee, Laurelvale and Portadown since early in 1927, seven double workings being usually provided.[10] The United Bus Service also worked between Portadown and Armagh, Portadown and Newry and served Ahorey.

The railway's last take-over in County Armagh occurred on 2 November 1931 when it acquired the services provided by T Nugent of Keady, together with his 14 buses (3 Dennis; 11 Vulcan). Nugent ran his first bus in May 1926 with which he opened a twice-daily service between Armagh and Keady and, within a year, he had increased this frequency to seven double workings on weekdays and two on Sundays. The business continued to grow and by the autumn of 1931 his buses were running between Armagh and Ballybay via Monaghan, as well as via Keady, and were also providing a service to Keady via Drumhillery. In their early days some of the Nugent buses carried conductresses[11] but this practice was vetoed by the government which ruled that, unless specially exempted by the Ministry of Home Affairs, all buses seating more than 14 passengers had to carry a male conductor. On the other hand, the authorities in Dublin seem to have raised no objection to the Gillan Bus Company of Sligo employing Mrs Margaret Gillan as one of its drivers; a vocation from which she retired in 1937 after many years of service.[12] In his first year as a bus operator Nugent had to face rivals on the roads between Armagh, Keady and Ballybay. The Keady bus was owned by a Portadown man named Williamson who, early in July 1927, changed his route to that between Armagh and Loughgall.[13] The Ballybay opposition was also short-lived; it was provided by F H Nelson of Ballybay[14] who, after a few months, transferred his attention to a more lucrative market by competing with the trams in the Belfast Bus War of 1928. In 1930 the railway itself applied for permission to run buses between Armagh and Keady but this was refused on the grounds that Nugent was already providing a satisfactory service. However, in the next year, the railway came to an agreement with Nugent to take over his buses and the operation of his road services on both sides of the border. In the south, Nugent's buses had been providing services between Ballybay and Carrickmacross, as well as between the latter and Cavan via Bailieborough and Cootehill.

Counties Donegal and Tyrone

The GNR made three acquisitions in Tyrone, namely the Dreadnought Motor Service which was owned by C H Donaghy of Omagh, the buses owned by Roberts Bros of Derry which ran between Strabane and Castlederg and the service which had been worked by D J Davidson of Aughnacloy between Dungannon and Monaghan via Aughnacloy.

77. GNR Dennis G bus Reg UI 2194 at Foyle Road, Derry, 12 July 1931. This 20-seater vehicle was built in 1929. Photographer A W Croughton. Courtesy B Boyle. UFTM L3779/16

Donaghy's first venture as a bus owner was in the winter of 1926/27 when he started a service between Omagh, Drumquin and Castlederg (see page 100); but it was so badly patronised that he soon changed his routes to one between Omagh, Strabane and Derry. Here he was more successful and, by November 1927 was providing four double workings between Omagh and Derry with four additional short workings between Strabane and Derry. The Strabane-Derry shuttle service had been opened earlier in the year by H Brook, who temporarily transferred one of his Pilot Buses from Portadown to Strabane to work it. After a few months he withdrew, thereby giving Donaghy a monopoly of the Derry-Strabane traffic. However, on 5 December 1927 Catherwood inaugurated a twice-daily service between Belfast and Derry via Armagh and Omagh[15] in which the 110 miles were scheduled to be covered in 5hr 35min. However, owing to lack of support on the northern part of the route, he withdrew his buses from going beyond Omagh early in 1928. Nevertheless, his published time-tables continued to give the times of his Belfast-Derry service, but stated that north of Omagh it would be worked by Donaghy's Dreadnought BS, a move which led to a rumour that Catherwood was contemplating a take-over of Donaghy's business. At about this time, Donaghy started a daily service between Omagh and Enniskillen, the schedules being arranged that passengers from Enniskillen had only to wait for a few minutes at Omagh for a bus to Derry, whereas in the opposite direction the connections were not so good! However, by the time that Donaghy had begun working to Enniskillen, W A Simpson's Fleetwing BS was already well established on the route and continued to run between Omagh and Enniskillen until the NIRTB take-

78. Robert Bros Lacre bus Reg UI 143 at Greencastle with R E Roberts at the wheel. It went into service in May 1912. This photograph was taken at the end of the first outward run. UFTM L1528/8

over. In the meantime, the six buses (2 Commer; 4 Gilford) owned by Donaghy had been taken over by the GNR on 20 June 1931. About three years before this, a third competitor appeared on the Omagh-Enniskillen Road in the role of the Dublin-owned Connemara Omnibus Service. On 1 April 1928 its buses began to provide a daily service between Dublin and Derry via Enniskillen and Omagh; but a year later they were withdrawn because their proprietors went into liquidation.

On 1 October 1926 Roberts Bros began to run a bus between Strabane, Sion Mills, Victoria Bridge and Castlederg, and shortly afterwards opened a service between Derry and Stranorlar via St Johnston and Raphoe.[16] On the Castlederg route they provided three double workings, two of which were extended to Killeter while on the Stranorlar service as many as six round workings were ultimately provided daily. In August 1930 the GNR acquired the six buses (3 Chevrolet; 2 Dennis; 1 Gilford) with which the Roberts had been operating their Castlederg and Stranorlar services. This purchase gave the railway direct access to parts of the Foyle Basin which had hitherto been on the fringe of the GNR catchment area.

79. GNR railbus E at Manorhamilton, 29 June 1938. This ADC vehicle was originally a Louth and Meath Omnibus Company roadbus Reg ZI 2452 and was converted in 1934. GF Egan, the mechanical engineer of the SLNCR lived in the house at the top of the photograph. Photographer H C Casserley. 41077.1741

80. GNR Leyland roadbus Reg ZA 3833 temporarily fitted with railway wheels for an exhibition at the Royal Dublin Society in 1934. It never ran on a railway. UFTM L3728/6.

In east Tyrone D J Davidson's buses had become well established by the summer of 1928, when they were scheduled to cover the 26 miles between Dungannon and Monaghan, via Aughnacloy, in 1hr 30min, passengers being daily. His timetable handouts, like those of practically all local bus operators in the province charged 3s single, 5s return. These compared favourably with 5s single by rail, a journey which took from 1hr 37min to 2hr 21min with a change of trains in Portadown. Davidson also ran a bus between Aughnacloy and Fintona, but this was always regarded as a subsidiary route compared with that between Dungannon and Monaghan on which three round trips were usually worked, carried advertisements. In Davidson's case, however, it seems that his conductors did more than merely collect fares for one advertisement for a particular brand of sausages contained the statement 'When in Monaghan, shop at Corrs, if you cannot get to Monaghan give your orders to the conductor.' Finally, Davidson's BS, together with his two 20-seater Dennis buses, became GNR property on 17 June 1932.

Counties Cavan and Monaghan

Altogether, the GNR acquired seven bus services operating in the counties of Cavan and Monaghan. In the summer of 1929 it took over the six buses (3 Dennis; 2 Reo; 1ADC) with which James Parkes of Castleblayney had been trading between Monaghan and Dundalk since

81. Magnet bus service. The vehicle is an Associated Daimler Co 416 bus Reg IZ 1755 with 32-seater body by Shorts. The woman in the photograph taken in 1929 is Mrs May Beattie, the driver's wife. Date, 1929. Courtesy Paul Rafferty. UFTM L3839/1

1926. His buses operated as the Classic BS and the majority of them were routed via Castleblayney and Carrickmacross and the remainder used the direct road through Cullaville, a total of eight double workings being usually provided. His buses competed very effectively with the railway since Monaghan and Dundalk are about 32 miles apart by road compared with 51 miles by rail. In the same year the railway took over the three ADC 30-seaters which Fairway of Dublin had been running between the capital and Monaghan. In 1931, the Nugent BS, the Kelvin BS and the Gordon BS all became railway property. The former had been on the road since 1928 and owned three International 20-seaters. The latter had been started by A W Gordon, the Ford dealer in Cavan, on 26 August 1925 under the name of the Magnet Bus Service which initially provided a twice daily service between Dublin and Cavan.[17] Shortly afterwards the services were extended to include Ballina and Longford. In 1927 the Bangor bus owners, Matthew and Norman Morrow, acquired a proprietary interest in the company and changed its name to A W Gordon (1928) Ltd. Three years later they sold their holding, which included five buses (3 ADC; 1 AEC; 1 Morris) to the GNR which, in due course, transferred them to the Irish Omnibus Company. At the time the Irish Omnibus Company was a subsidiary of the Great Southern Railways (later Córas Iompair Éireann) and the sharing was in accord with an agreement between the GNR and GSR that each would restrict its omnibus activities to north and south respectively of a line between Dublin and Sligo. Since the Dublin-Cavan buses ran along this arbitrary boundary, it was agreed to work them as a joint undertaking. The fifth company to join the railway was Phair Bros of Belturbet who, at the time of the merger, owned five buses varying in age between four and seven years. The Phairs owned a garage and ran a bus service between Cavan and Enniskillen via Swanlinbar which, in 1928, was providing two double workings on weekdays when the 40 mile journey (11 miles of which were in Northern Ireland) was scheduled to take about 2hr 15min. In December of the same year the Phairs arranged that some of their buses would

82. GNR Leyland Lion LT 2 Reg AZ 7643 at GNR goods yard Grosvenor Road, Belfast. The bodywork was built by Stewarts of Scotland in 1931. Photographer A R Hogg. R Ludgate Collection. UFTM L3773/12

connect at Cavan with some of the Gordon buses thereby enabling passengers to travel by road from Enniskillen to Dublin. The bus journey was advertised to take about seven hours compared with 3hr 30min by train but the single bus fare was 12s 6d compared with 16s 11d by rail. In 1929 the Phair Bros received permission from the Northern Ireland government to re-open a service between Enniskillen and Longford which had been started a year or so earlier by W E White of Enniskillen (see page 95). White owned a 14-seater Chevrolet which, during its few months of activity, used the same route between Enniskillen and Swanlinbar as the buses belonging to the Phairs and made two round trips each day being scheduled to go from Enniskillen to Longford in 2hr 30min. Unfortunately, White's bus was badly damaged in an accident in August 1929, after which his service was never resumed. On the other hand, the Phairs decided not to take up the licence offered to them to work this route. The last service to be taken over by the railway was the Boyd BS of Clones.[18] This company had been providing four double workings between Clones and Monaghan since the early 1930s, its buses covering the 13 miles in 40 minutes, the fares being 1s 3d single, and 1s 9d return. When the railway first considered the service for purchase in 1936, it discovered the company possessed only one bus, a 1929 20-seater Reo which had been bought from the Tonic BS, Bangor, for £40! Nevertheless, two years later the GNR took over the working of the route.

In 1933 the Dublin government passed an act[19] whereby the majority of the road services in the Free State would be operated by the railways. As a result of this, Catherwood's Dublin-Cork service was transferred to the IOC and his other services south of the border were taken over by the GNR on 29 November 1933. Earlier in the same year the GNR had obtained a contract to run buses between the County Donegal Railways termini at Killybegs and Glenties, as the four buses which the CDR had purchased to work this service were in such a deplorable condition that they had to be immediately taken off the road.

In the days when the GNR operated road passenger services, its buses were under the control

83. GNR Dennis Lancet bus Reg AZ 9633 fitted with a 30 seater Weymann body supplied new in 1932. Courtesy B Boyle. UFTM L3779/9

of the company's road service manager who reported to the traffic manager. The first holder of the post was Alexander Hutchinson who eventually had two senior assistants; one was stationed at Enniskillen and the other in Dundalk where all major repairs were carried out. The railway had begun its road services with a very mixed fleet but this was being slowly remedied by restricting new purchases to Albions, AECs and Leylands. An exception was made for the four special Leyland TS2 32-seaters which were acquired jointly with the NCC in 1930 for use in top-class touring, they were painted in GNR colours and carried the names of their joint owners on their sides. When it became apparent that the railway would have to withdraw its road services from Northern Ireland, it transferred its Leylands to the Free State and their place was taken by comparatively new 30-seater Albion and Dennis buses. Nevertheless, about half of the 50 buses transferred by the GNR to the NIRTB on 1 October 1935 had, at one time or another, belonged to Northern Ireland operators who had, themselves, been taken over by the railway between 1929 and 1932. The GNR bus livery was dark blue and cream with the company's crest and name on each side of the body; wheels and mudguards were black. Finally, like all other members of the 'Big Five,' the GNR received NIRTB stocks instead of cash for its road services in Northern Ireland, the number of stocks being 39,763.

84. GNR/NCC Leyland TS 3 bus Reg AZ 9135. This 24-seater coach was supplied new in 1932. Courtesy B Boyle. UFTM L3780/5

85. GNR brochure showing cross-country tours, 1936 UFTM

REFERENCES

1 *Newry Telegraph,* 10 June 1913; 12 July 1913
2 *Newry Reporter,* 23 May 1916
3 Carlingford Bay and County Down (London: Norton and Shaw, 1878)
4 *Mourne Observer,* 1 March 1952
5 *Newry Reporter,* 3 August 1916
6 *Belfast Topics,* August–December 1927
7 *Belfast Telegraph,* 21 July 1926
8 *Armagh Guardian,* 19 March 1926
9 *Newry Reporter,* 28 January 1926
10 Poster, Armagh County Museum
11 *Armagh Guardian,* 5 August 1927
12 *Irish Independent,* 4 September 1937
13 *Armagh Guardian,* 6 July 1927; 30 July 1927
14 *Northern Standard,* 26 August 1927; *Armagh Guardian,* 16 September 1927
15 *Armagh Guardian,* 16 December 1927
16 *Londonderry Sentinel,* 2 October 1926
17 Smyth, T S, The Civic History of the town of Cavan (Dublin, 1938) p. 126
18 *Communication,* Cyril McIntyre, Dublin
19 Road Traffic Act No. 11, 29 June 1933

6. Northern Counties Committee

In the 1930s the London Midland and Scottish Railway operated bus services in Counties Antrim and Derry which covered a route mileage of about 565 miles, about double that of its railway track in Northern Ireland. The LMS got its first footing in Ulster in July 1903 when the Midland Railway purchased the Belfast and Northern Counties Railway which had been running trains between Belfast, Derry, Larne and Portrush for the previous 40 years. The Midland ran its Irish subsidiary through a committee known as the Northern Counties Committee, and this arrangement was continued when the Midland became part of the LMS at the amalgamation of 1923, when all the major railway companies in Britain were merged into four groups. The NCC and its predecessor, had been running road services since the late 1880s but did not become a large-scale operator in this field until after the passing of the Railway (Road Vehicles) NI Act[1] in 1927. It then began to buy out its competitors and, by the end of 1934, had taken over the businesses of 17 private operators who had hitherto been running buses in what was considered to be NCC territory. However, it failed to get possession of the services worked by its largest competitor, HMS Catherwood, who retained his independence until he, and all the other road operators working entirely within Northern Ireland, were compulsorily merged with the NIRTB in 1935. As a result of which the railway was compensated by receiving stocks in the new organisation, no cash payment being involved in the transaction.

The Belfast and Northern Counties Railway was the first railway in the British Isles, to use mechanically-propelled vehicles for passenger road services. On 1 April 1902 it began to operate two Thornycroft 14-seater, 24 horse power, steam omnibuses on short runs from Greenisland station to the Lough Shore at Whiteabbey, Sea Park and Silverstream. The vehicles, which together cost £1500, were chain-driven with spoked wheels fitted with narrow iron tyres and passengers sat facing one another as in a wagonette.[2] In one a rudimentary shelter was provided by a roof but there were no side curtains to shelter passengers from driving rain, whereas the other had glassed windows. Unfortunately, the buses cut up the roads so badly that they were withdrawn in 1908 and replaced by horse-drawn wagonettes, somewhat similar to those used when the service started in the mid-1880s. In January 1924, the NCC substituted a 24-seater Ford charabanc on the route but this was withdrawn in November 1925 due to competition from other buses which, by then, had begun to work from Whiteabbey and other places on the Shore Road to Belfast. However, this was not the first occasion in which a passenger-carrying mechanically-propelled vehicle ran on the roads of County Antrim. On 1 January 1836, a steam carriage seating at least 16 passengers travelled from Doagh to Belfast where it was placed on display for a few days. As it passed through the streets of Belfast it was preceded by a military band. The coach had been built by John Rowan of Doagh, an iron foundry owner who had spent five years on the project. It was powered by a two-cylindered engine with a tubular boiler and it was claimed it reached a speed of 15 mph on a level road.[3]

In August 1905 the NCC acquired two Thornycroft petrol-driven charabancs which it used on tours from the company's hotel at Portrush. Some months later one of the charabancs was fitted with an enclosed body and employed in ferrying passengers between the narrow-gauge railway terminus at Parkmore and the seaside villages of Waterfoot and Cushendall.[4] Neither the road nor the vehicle was sufficiently robust for all-year-round workings and, in March 1907, the NCC arranged with Henry McNeill Ltd of Larne to run a horse-drawn wagonette over the route for which, after 1915, they received an annual subsidy of £100 from the railway.[5] In 1928 McNeill withdrew from the contract which was then given to J Boyd of Parkmore who had been running a 14-seater motor charabanc from Parkmore since April 1926. The journey usually took about half an hour and a single fare cost 1s 3d, but passengers could obtain through Third Class tickets from Cushendall to Ballymena for

86. MR NCC Thornycroft charabancs Reg IA 123 and IA 124 at Garron Tower Hotel, Co Antrim. They entered service in August 1905. Ulster Museum Welch Collection

2s 3d single or 3s 6d return. Boyd continued to meet all trains at Parkmore until the withdrawal of passenger services from the branch in September 1930.

On 1 October 1919 the NCC, in response to local demand, inaugurated a motor bus service between Ballymena and Portglenone. Initially it was worked by two 45-horse power AEC buses but, after three years, it was closed down due to intense competition from privately-owned motor cars. These car owners had found that a few coppers from those picked up en route made a worthwhile contribution to the cost of their petrol which, in those days, was about 2s per gallon.

The passing of the Railways (Road Vehicles) NI Act in 1927 permitted railway companies in Northern Ireland to run road services under conditions somewhat similar to those enjoyed by private operators. The NCC, with the financial resources of the LMS behind it, was able to take full advantage of the act. In 1929 it began a vigorous policy by which it planned to build up a transport monopoly throughout its territory thereby hoping to achieve substantial economies, such as the withdrawal of unremunerative passenger services from branch lines. Ten private undertakings were acquired in 1929, five in 1930 and one each in 1932 and 1934, thereby giving a total of 126 buses taken over at a total cost of about £150,000.

87. NCC Leyland PLSC2 bus Reg XI 7874 at Portstewart railway station. The vehicle is fitted with a Leyland 31-seater body and was supplied new to BOC in 1927. Courtesy B Boyle. UFTM L3780/12

The railway's first purchase was made on 29 July 1929 when the three Dennis buses, which Hugh R Martin had been running on a fixed-interval hourly service between Belfast, Carrickfergus and Kilroot, were taken over. At the time his buses were scheduled to cover the 14 miles to Belfast in 45 minutes, the fares charged being 9d single and 1s 3d return. The NCC continued to provide a similar service, and followed the precedent of other major road operators by providing a morning and evening shuttle service between its Belfast terminal and the shipyards, regular patrons being charged 6d per week for this twice daily facility.

The next service to be taken over was that of Hugh Abernethy and Sons who 'had brought the bus to Ballyclare'. In 1922 this company began running a Lancia bus between Ballyclare and Belfast and, by 1927, it was providing six double workings to the City via Doagh and eight via Lisnalinchy. A feature to the service was the issue of Six Double Journey Tickets' at 5s 6d, whereas

88. Flack's Lough Neagh Queen *Reo bus Reg XI 7342 outside John Hill's Motor Agency, Seymour Street, Belfast, c1924. The body was built by Harkness of Belfast. UFTM L3745/11*

89. Flack's Albion bus Reg AZ 604 with taxi and trams at Royal Avenue, Belfast. This bus was purchased by Belfast Corporation at the termination of the Belfast bus war in 1928. UFTM L3237/8

the cost of six ordinary return tickets was 9s. Abernethy's seven buses, which varied in size from an 18-seater Dennis to a 35-seater Gotfredson became NCC property on 19 August 1929. On 10 September of the same year the 20-seater Reo, named *Lough Neagh Queen*, which Hugh Flack of Coagh was using on a once-daily service between Cookstown and Belfast, was also taken over when its owner received £690 in compensation for his bus and service. Flack had gone onto the route in 1925 and, throughout the mid-1920s had to face severe competition from the McGuckens, who also came from the Cookstown area, but had merged with the BOC in 1927.

In October 1929 the NCC acquired the majority of local services which operated between Coleraine and the seaside resorts of Portrush and Portstewart. Some of these commenced running in 1924 when Wallace Kennedy of Portrush and Peter Doherty, who owned the Anchor Bar in Portstewart, began to run motor charabancs between their home towns and Coleraine, both proprietors charging their patrons 6d for a single journey and 9d return. During the summer of the same year Kennedy commenced a shuttle service along the coast road between Portrush and Coleraine and in the autumn opened a service between Coleraine and Castlerock.[6] Shortly afterwards he began running a bus between Coleraine and Kilrea on which the 14 mile journey was timed to take 50 minutes. In the summer of 1929 the Kennedy buses which were, by that time, owned by his widow, Mrs Rachel Kennedy, were providing a half-hourly service between Portrush and Coleraine and those of Doherty, which ran under the name of 'Anchor Motors' were working a similar service to and from Portstewart. At their take-over by the railway Mrs Kennedy owned seven buses (1 Bean; 2 Leyland; 4 Dennis) and Doherty possessed three Dennis 17/19-seaters.

Three other proprietors in the Coleraine area also sold their undertakings to the NCC in October 1929. The first was the Bann Motor Service Co Ltd[7] which, in the summer of 1926, began to run buses between Coleraine and Magherafelt. Within a year, it was providing four double workings to Magherafelt together with a subsidiary service between Garvagh and Ballymena via Kilrea and Rasharkin. The latter service, together with one Lancia was sold to Catherwood in January 1929; but the Magherafelt service and its associated buses (1 Daimler; 1 Lancia; 1 Reo) were acquired by the NCC in the same year. The next service to be taken over was that run by Stewart Bros of Garvagh whose two 20-seater Reo buses had plied between Coleraine and Maghera. After the sale, the Stewarts moved to Portrush and continued in the private-hire and touring businesses until both these sectors of their organisation, along with their four buses (3 Thornycroft; 1 Leyland), were taken over by the NIRTB six years later. By this time they had completed 21 years in the motor trade, having obtained their first Charabanc in 1915, a vehicle often referred to as the *Royal Red Open Charabanc.*[8] The third proprietor was John McDonald who opened a service between Coleraine, Dervock and Ballycastle on 26 July 1926. During the next year he expanded his business by working between Portrush and Ballycastle. For the next 37 years, these services were provided first by the NCC, then by the NIRTB, followed by the UTA which, on 25 April 1966, handed over their provision to the locally owned Coastal Bus Service Ltd. However, after about eight years, changes in the economic climate led to the working of the routes being returned to the public sector and, since 10 March 1974, Services Nos 171 and 172 of Ulsterbus now work between Coleraine and Ballycastle and between Portrush and Ballycastle respectively.

Two more services were acquired late in 1929. Both ran to Dungiven, one from Derry and the other from Limavady. The former was the oldest motor bus service to run entirely in County Londonderry having been started by Roberts Bros of Derry in 1912. The latter was operated by Hutchinson Bros of Limavady and followed roughly the same route as the Dungiven Branch of the railway. It had been purchased by the NCC with the intention that its acquisition would enable it to withdraw passenger services from the branch but, while the bus service was taken over in October 1929, passenger trains continued to run between Limavady and Dungiven until January 1933.

90. NCC Leyland Lion bus converted into a railbus but retaining its road fleet No. 42 and Reg CH 7910. Courtesy Real Photographs. UFTM L3800/14

The railway's first acquisition in 1930 was completed on 17 February when it acquired three 14-seater buses (1 Chevrolet; 2 Morris) which Alexander Frizzell of Portstewart had been using for touring and for operating a shuttle service along the coast road between Portstewart and Portrush during the summer since the mid-1920s. The next was on 26 March when the NCC made its largest and most important acquisition by taking over the 59 buses with which the BOC had been operating its services in north-east Ulster. Twelve of the routes acquired terminated in Belfast and the remaining ones worked from either Ballymena or Larne. All had been started by private operators who had been taken over by the BOC during the intervening years. Brief descriptions of the workings of these formerly privately owned services are given in Chapter 3.

91. Erskines Leyland PLSC1 bus Reg XI 7810. It was supplied new in 1927 with a 31-seater Leyland body. The driver pictured is Tom Black. UFTM L1528/2

In the same week as that of the BOC acquisition, the NCC got possession of the services worked by Joseph McNeilly of Belfast. McNeilly had been a proprietor of the Princess Bus Service but had resigned shortly after its merger with the BOC in April 1927. About a year later he began to run buses in competition with the trams in Belfast. When this practice had to stop due to a change in the public transport regulations, he sold two of the three buses which he had been using on the service to the Belfast Corporation and leased the third to Alexander Moore of the Wellington BS in Ballymena. At the time Moore was providing at least two double workings between Ballymena and Belfast which followed somewhat circuitous routes; one going via Glenwhirry and Ballyclare and the other through Kells and Doagh. He was also running a twice daily service between Ballymena and Cushendall via Parkmore. In February 1929 McNeilly took over the Wellington BS and three months later acquired the bus service belonging to S & J Erskine of Ballyclare which had been running between Ballyclare and Belfast since 1926. The Erskine fleet consisted of four 31-seater Leyland buses which were painted blue and carried names such as *King of the Road* and *Queen of the Road.* At the time they were providing a total of 11 double workings on weekdays with 15 on Saturdays, some going via Doagh and others via Lisnalinchy. Immediately after this takeover, McNeilly increased the frequency of the workings to Belfast, and, by Christmas 1929, was operating an hourly service between Ballyclare and the city as well as two double workings between Belfast and Cushendun via Ballymena. In March 1931 he disposed of his eight buses to the NCC (6 Leyland; 1 Gilford; 1 AEC). Joseph McNeilly was an uncompromising and efficient road service operator who, within a few months of taking over the Wellington BS, had forced a rival operator, named John Mawhinney, off the route between Parkgate

92. McNeill's Daimler wagonette at the King's Arms Hotel, Larne, Monday, 20 June 1898. This was probably the first motor vehicle for hire in Ulster. The man in the bowler hat is Henry McNeill. Courtesy Larne Folklore Society. UFTM L437/11

and Kells. He also transformed the Ballyclare service from a rural bus route to a fixed-interval suburban service. After selling out to the railway he moved to North Down where he took over the businesses of two small operators (McCreight and Ross; William Scott), who ran buses in the Drumbo area, and continued to work these until the formation of the NIRTB.

In April 1930 the NCC acquired the buses and charabancs owned by the long-established firm of Henry McNeill Ltd of Larne. This was one of the oldest road transport and hotel undertakings in Ireland. It had been founded by Henry McNeill in 1853, a man of character who is reputed to have

WHEN TOURING THE ANTRIM COAST
CALL AT ANY OF
McNEILL'S HOTELS
For Luncheon, Dinner or Tea.
CHARGES MODERATE.

KING'S ARMS and CASTLE SWEENEY HOTELS, McNEILL'S HOTEL, MAIN STREET, LARNE. GARRON TOWER HOTEL, GARRONPOINT.

Day Excursion Parties specially catered for.
Dining accommodation for 500.

Organisers of Pic-nic Parties, Works, Outings, etc., should write for particulars to HENRY McNEILL, Ltd.
W. B. LEGG, Managing Director.

been the first person to operate package tours in Ireland. At the turn of the century he owned several hotels and a large posting establishment which provided horse-drawn outside cars to take his guests to Glenariff and other places of interest in the vicinity. His more adventurous patrons could hire his Daimler wagonette which was probably the first motor vehicle to be available for hire in Ulster. It could seat seven passengers, in addition to the driver. On its 'show the press' trip to Garron Tower on Monday 20 June 1898 it set off from McNeill's Kings Arms Hotel in Larne at 1130 hrs and after travelling at about 15 miles per hour got to within a mile of Glenarm when one of its driving chains came off.[9] This seems to have caused little delay and the party arrived at McNeill's Sea View Hotel at Garron Tower in time for lunch. In addition to touring, McNeill worked an all-year horse drawn long-car service for mail and passengers via the coast road from Larne to Cushendall, as well as from the latter to the railway station at Parkmore. During the summer of 1911 some of the long cars were replaced by motor charabancs. In 1915 he augmented his motor fleet by purchasing the two Thornycroft charabancs, which had been acquired by the NCC in 1905 and, during the 1920s, gradually

93. Henry McNeill's Commer charabanc Reg RI 3085, c1919. The registration number was a Dublin issue. UFTM L755/7

built up a fleet of about a dozen motor buses and charabancs of seven different makes, many of which were past their best, three still had solid tyres, when he sold the transport part of his business to the NCC in 1930. After this he continued as a package-tour operator but his patrons were taken on their coach trips in chartered buses.

The fifth operator to be taken over in 1930 was Robert Agnew of Portglenone who had been running buses between Portglenone and Ballymena since the withdrawal of the railway buses in 1922. Seven years later his business had expanded to include services from Portglenone to Magherafelt

94. Dennis, Ford and Maudslay buses at the Laharna Hotel, Larne, Co Antrim, c1920. The Maudslay bus was owned by Robinson's, Harbour Garage, Larne. UFTM L2148/2

95. *NCC Leyland Tiger TS6 bus Reg CZ 4818 on private hire work at the Laharna Hotel, Larne, c1935. There is also a BOC parcels van in the photograph. Courtesy B Boyle. UFTM L3781/11*

and from Randalstown to Belfast. On 25 April 1930, when the railway bought him out, he was the owner of four small buses (2 Dennis; 1 Dodge; 1 Guy).

The last two services to be taken over by the NCC were owned by Robert Strahan of Islandmagee and John C Mewhirter who, at the time, lived in Belfast. The former had been using a model T Ford to carry passengers between the railway station at Ballycarry and Islandmagee since 1923; he replaced this car by a bus in July 1926 and by the summer of 1928 was providing ten double workings between the station at Ballycarry and Portmuck. His buses were advertised as the Island Bus Service and connected with the principal trains. Through rail and bus tickets were issued from stations on the NCC to destinations in Islandmagee, a third class ticket from Belfast to Portmuck costing 2s single and 3s return. By 1932 his business had expanded to warrant the use of four buses (1 De Dion Bouton; 2 Dodge; 1 Gilford) and in June of that year he sold out to the railway for £2000, £500 of which was for goodwill. However, some nine years before this he had begun to carry worshippers to and from the First and Second Presbyterian Churches in Islandmagee, but these arrangements were upset in 1929 when the Ministry of Home Affairs inadvertently permitted the BOC to run a rival church bus to the two meeting-houses. After a few weeks the Government realised its mistake and rescinded its permission thereby restoring the Strahan monopoly. Nevertheless, Strahan had been so incensed by the arrival of an outsider, that he refused to carry anyone who had patronised the BOC. This action drew a government rebuke pointing out that, since he was a licensed public service operator, he had no choice in the selection of his passengers and, furthermore, unless he stopped this discrimination immediately he would be banned from the road.

On 31 March 1934 the NCC made its last acquisition by purchasing the two buses (Dennis; Reo) which John C Mewhirter had been running between Parkgate and Belfast via Templepatrick and Hydepark. The service had been started by John Mawhinney in 1925 and by the time it had been finally acquired by the NCC it had passed through the hands of three other operators (R Dow, W Dow, J C Mewhirter). By the summer of 1928 Mawhinney was providing eleven double workings over this 14 mile route, the journey being advertised to take 50 minutes. Two of the runs were subsequently extended to Kells but these were withdrawn in August 1929 due to competition from Joseph McNeilly's buses which ran over this part of the route on their way from Ballymena to Belfast via Kells and Doagh. Some twelve months later, Belfast Rural District Council began to voice complaints about the unreliability of the Mawhinney buses and in March 1932 he sold his two vehicles (Reo; Thornycroft) to Robert Dow of Belfast for £1200. Eight months later Robert's brother William who had taken over the buses in the intervening period, sold them to J C Mewhirter for the same sum. The new owner, who also managed the local town bus service in Larne on behalf of W A Agnew, a director of HMS Catherwood, continued to run between Belfast and Parkgate until the purchase of his buses by the NCC in the spring of 1934.

The acquisitions of 1929-34 had given the railway not only a fleet of assorted buses but also a

96. NCC Albion Valkyrie PX65 bus Reg CZ 2017 beside the Church of Ireland church in York Road, Belfast, c1934. Courtesy B Boyle. UFTM L3781/6

staff comprising individuals brought up in very different traditions. Furthermore, several of the owners had never paid much attention to maintaining their buses in sound mechanical condition so that, in its early days as a road service operator, the NCC had more than its fair share of mechanical failures and complaints about the poor service provided. In addition, some of the smaller operators had allowed local worthies such as the police, postmen, local government officials and their relatives to travel free, unofficial concessions which caused storms of protest when they were withdrawn by the NCC. Complaints were also continually being received by the Ministry of Home Affairs about the poor services provided in certain areas, one correspondent writing 'It is evidently the intention of the railway company to run the service to suit themselves and not the public.' Finally, in July 1930 the Ministry wrote a very firm letter to the railway about the inadequate services it was providing in a certain district which ended with the following words; 'indicates clearly that the local supervision of the service provided is inadequate and unsatisfactory ... the Ministry will be obliged to reconsider the question of allowing some other operator to provide the necessary service.' The rivalry which existed between the railway buses and those owned by HMS Catherwood was keen, especially at bus crew level. Drivers would jostle one another and race to be the first at bus stops, and conductors engaged in over-enthusiastic touting for passengers.

Indeed, the position became so serious that both operators received a communication from the government pointing out that their 'staffs must act properly'.

Early in 1931 Major Malcolm S Spier, who had been the Assistant General Superintendent of the LMS in Glasgow, was appointed to manage the NCC. Soon order began to replace chaos on the company's road services. Later in the same year the NCC issued bus crews with uniforms. These were based on railway practice with inspectors having gold braid on their caps and conductors dressed similarly to ticket collectors; the main difference between the uniforms of its rail and road staffs was that bus drivers wore breeches and leggings. Also in 1931, the company introduced recognised bus stops on the Shore Road in Belfast; hitherto, throughout the whole of Ulster, buses had stopped anywhere on request to pick up or set down passengers. Another innovation brought in at about this time was the extension of the validity of season tickets which became interchangeable between road and rail, probably the first time that this facility had been given to season ticket holders in the British Isles.

97. NCC Leyland Lion LT2 bus Reg AZ 5673 at Smithfield bus depot, Belfast in the early 1930s. Courtesy B Boyle. UFTM L3780/15

In its early days as a road passenger operator, the NCC had been handicapped in that its buses terminated at the kerb side in different parts of Belfast, thus buses for Cookstown terminated in College Square, for Kilrea at Frederick Street and those going to Ballyclare in Ormeau Avenue. The opening of a central bus depot in Smithfield on 1 November 1930 ended

98. NCC Smithfield bus depot, Belfast, May 1931. The builders are laying concrete floors. The 220 ft. long depot could house 40 buses in the main bay. Photographer A R Hogg. Courtesy W Montgomery. UFTM L3781/2

99. NCC Leyland breakdown lorry, c1932. The building in the background belonged to W W Kennedy & Co, Carriers and Removal Contractors, Belfast. UFTM L3313/7

this inconvenience and the travelling public were facilitated still further when the GNR buses began to use the same terminal a year later. Early in 1931 the railway opened a central garage in Duncrue Street, Belfast, which was considered to be one of the most up-to-date workshops of its kind in Ireland.[10] It could accommodate over 40 buses and had the necessary facilities for carrying out all major repairs to the company's fleet. At about the same time the NCC raised the status of its road manager to that of Road Superintendent with direct access to Major Spier; the first holder of the office was George Madden who, unfortunately, had to retire, after only a few years in office, due to ill health.

100. NCC Leyland Tiger TS6 bus Reg CZ 4818 at Delargy's Hotel and Motor Garage, Cushendall, Co Antrim, c1935. Courtesy B Boyle. UFTM L3781/13

101. NCC Leyland LT2 bus Reg AZ 5620 at Coleraine in the early 1930s. Courtesy B Boyle. UFTM L1528/3

The busiest route operated by the NCC was that between Belfast and Carrickfergus with over 45 double workings on weekdays. There was often overcrowding on this route, especially on Monday mornings, when some of the workings had to be provided with two or more buses. Other busy routes were those to Ballyclare and Ballymena with about 25 double workings on each. On the latter, the railway buses competed with those belonging to HMS Catherwood. Seven double workings ran to Larne, some via Carrickfergus and others via Ballyclare and, in summer, there were also seven return workings to Cushendun which was served either via Ballyclare and Larne or via Ballymena and Parkmore. Adequate services were provided in Bann Side and, during the summer NCC buses ran several times each hour along the coast road between Portstewart and Portrush. From Derry seven double workings were usually run to Limavady and to Dungiven, routes on which the buses of HMS Catherwood provided rival services. On Sundays a much reduced service was usually worked except, that during the summer, additional buses would be run to seaside resorts such as Portrush, Portstewart and Ballycastle.

During its six years as a large road passenger service operator, the NCC took steps to standardise its fleet by purchasing mainly Leyland and Albion 32-seaters. All its buses were painted in Midland red, the same colour as its railway carriages, with white roofs and black mudguards and with the name 'Northern Counties' on their sides. At the time of the merger with the NIRTB, the NCC was the second largest passenger road operator in the province and owned 131 buses, all of which were single deckers.

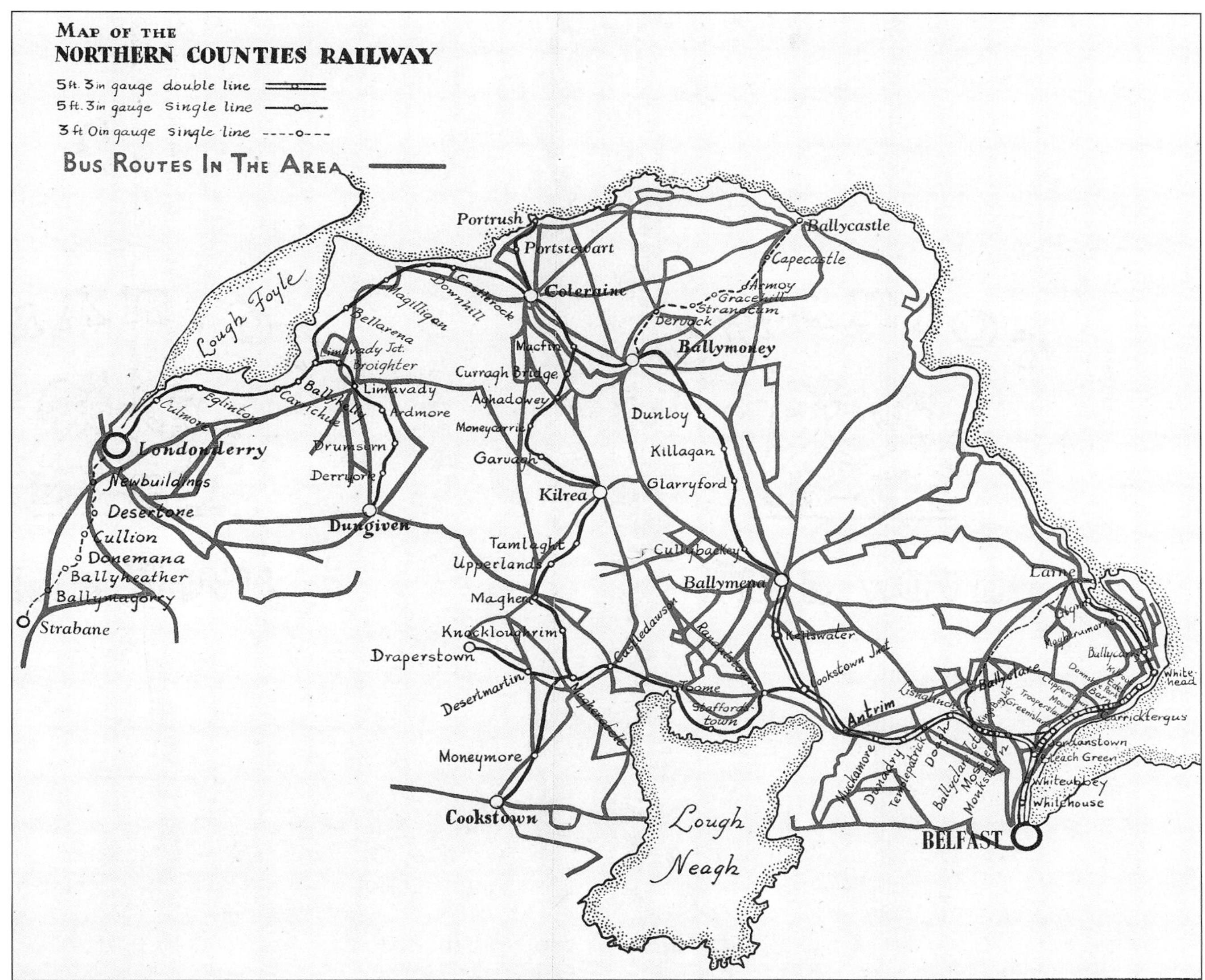

102. Map of NCC railway and bus routes in 1934. UFTM L3713/9

REFERENCES

1 Railways (Road Vehicles) NI Act, 17 & 18 Geo V c9, 31 May 1927
2 B&NCR Board Minutes, June 1902
3 Moore, J, *Motor Makers of Ireland*, p 104 (Belfast 1982)
4 NCC Board Minutes, June 1905 – March 1907
5 NCC Board Minutes, July – September 1915
6 *Coleraine Chronicle*, 8 November 1924
7 *Coleraine Chronicle*, 24 July 1926, PRONI COM40/2/390/1
8 Mullin, T H, *Coleraine in Modern Times*, p 64 (Belfast 1979)
9 *Larne Times*, 25 June 1898
10 *Irish Engineering News*, March 1931

General:

Currie, JRL The Northern Counties Railway, Vol 2, Appendix 5 (Newton Abbot 1974)

7. Northern Ireland Road Transport Board

The act for the formation of the Northern Ireland Road Transport Board was passed on 16 July 1935 and during the autumn of the same year the board took over the buses and the routes of over 60 different bus operators. This chapter deals mainly with those companies which remained independent until the formation of the NIRTB.

County Antrim

Nineteen omnibus proprietors in Antrim never joined either HMS Catherwood or the NCC. Four of these provided services to Belfast, four worked in the Larne area and the remainder traded in the neighbourhood of Ballymena and Coleraine. The largest was the Independent Bus Service which ultimately owned eight Leylands, and eight of the others possessed only one or two buses.

The five main companies serving Belfast were the Independent Bus Service, the Aldergrove Motor Service, Windsor Bus Service, Woodburn Bus Service and Larne's Pride.

The Independent BS began to operate between Belfast, Magherafelt and Draperstown on 1 June 1928 and, by the end of the next year, was providing at least seven double workings to and from Belfast. In the spring of 1929 the government permitted some of its buses to extend their runs to Dungiven and, on 27 July 1929, they began to work the Belfast-Dungiven service. Here they connected with buses belonging to Roberts Bros which, at the time, ran between Dungiven and Derry, thereby enabling passengers to travel conveniently and very cheaply by bus from Belfast to Derry, the monthly return fare being 10s 9d compared with 27s 8d by rail. However, no information seems to be available as to how many connections were missed, for throughout its life the Independent BS was continually in trouble with the authorities for changing routes without prior approval, for altering timetables without adequate notice and for cutting fares; indeed, on several occasions it was warned that its operating licence would be revoked unless such behaviour ceased. It was generally believed that its manager, H A Johnston of Comber, had a controlling interest in the business, but after the Independent BS had become incorporated as a private limited company on 26 July 1932, it was revealed that its principal shareholders were members of the Bell family who, at one time, had been associated with the Paragon BS which had run buses between Magherafelt and Belfast. In the autumn of 1933 the Bells transferred all their holding to Robert W Bell, a former joint-proprietor of the Paragon BS and who, when his company had joined the BOC in 1928, had undertaken not to run buses over any route previously worked by him for at least five years. The change in status to a limited company made little difference to the day-to-day working of the Independent BS which continued to operate in the Magherafelt area until the NIRTB took over its eight Leyland buses on 1 November 1935, after which shareholders had to wait until 1938 before receiving their compensation.

In 1926 David Wilson of Crumlin began to run a bus between the English Post Office at Aldergrove and Carlisle Circus in Belfast via Clady Corner and the Horse Shoe Road. By the summer of 1928 his service, which was known as the Aldergrove Motor Service, was providing three double workings over this route with additional workings on Saturdays and Sundays, the 18-mile journey taking about an hour. Like other operators in Ulster he carried children at half price but insisted that, when buses were crowded, children occupying a seat would have to pay full fare. He also ran a bus from Clady Corner to Antrim on Antrim fair days and was involved in private-hire work. When his business was taken over by the NIRTB he owned three buses (1 Albion; 2 Reo) and was providing four double workings between Aldergrove and Belfast.

The Windsor BS was formed by William Patterson in 1926 and, at first, provided four double workings between Belfast and Aghalee via Lisburn, Brookhill and Ballinderry. A year later he abandoned this route in favour of one between Belfast, Pond Park and Stoneyford Village, with some workings being extended to Lisburn on

103. Aldergrove Motor Service Albion bus Reg GE 9987. This bus, dating from 1930, was owned by David Wilson of Crumlin, Co Antrim. UFTM L1529/6

market days. Later he became involved in the Belfast Bus War. He attempted to continue operating in the city after the Bus War ended in December 1928, an action for which his operating licence was suspended. After several months it was restored but, by then, he had lost his enthusiasm for buses and, in September 1929, sold his business to his brother Robert who lived in Belfast. Robert, not only restored his brother's original services, which now included three double workings between Belfast and Stoneyford via Glen Road and Collinstown, but also purchased the Woodburn BS from Robert Dow in 1932. This provided three workings between Belfast and Lisburn via Stockman's Lane, Suffolk and Derriaghy. It had been started by A S Baird and S H Weir in 1926 under the name of the Suffolk Bus Service. In 1930 they disposed of it to R Dow, who apparently changed its name to the Woodburn BS and, under this name, Robert Patterson operated his now enlarged bus company until its take over by the NIRTB when his five buses (1 AEC; 4 Dennis) changed ownership at a cost of £12,300, but he had to wait for payment until the winter of 1938/39. One of the Patterson brothers owned the *Larne's Pride*, a bus which provided three round workings between Belfast and Larne via Carrickfergus in the summer of 1926.

In the mid-1920s James McAllister ran a service between Larne and Cushendun with an old and decrepit Ford charabanc which was in such a poor condition that it was condemned in 1929. Its replacement was a 14-seater FIAT, which dated from 1911, and had the greatest of difficulty in working even one round trip per day. This meant that its owner had frequently to borrow transport from Richard Barkley and William Irvine, both of whom ran buses in the Larne area. The former owned two small charabancs which, in August

1928, were providing two double workings between Larne and Cairncastle and eight round trips between Larne and Magheramorne. The latter were run for the benefit of the operatives at Magheramorne Cement Works, the first run of the day being timed to leave Larne at 0530 hrs. In 1932 the NCC applied to the government for permission to run over this route but its application was refused on the grounds that, although Barkley's buses were old, they provided an adequate and punctual service. Irvine, on the other hand, owned several garages in Larne and was interested mainly in private-hire and touring.[1] All three – Barkley, Irvine and McAllister – retained their independence until the NIRTB takeover; by which time McAllister had moved to Carrickfergus where he had become quite active in private-hire work, owning two very old Leyland and Renault charabancs for which the NIRTB paid him £950; Barkley received £1300 for the goodwill of his business and his 15-seater Crossley, whereas Irvine got £5000 in cash and 11,000 in stock for his two Dennis buses and his motor businesses in Larne. The fourth Larne operator was W A Agnew who was an executive director of HMS Catherwood Ltd, and the owner of Auto-Rolls, a company which hired out Rolls Royce taxis. In 1931 he obtained authority to run a town bus service in Larne. He also applied to run similar services in Bangor, Lisburn and Portadown but these were disallowed by the government. At Larne he appointed John C Mewhirter to be his local manager but the latter resigned in November 1932 to start his own bus service between Belfast and Parkgate. At the NIRTB takeover Agnew owned two small Commer buses which he had used on his local services in Larne.

104. W A Agnew's Commer Centaur bus Reg. IA 9987 at Larne with driver, A Block and conductor, A Burns, c1932. Agnew later became one of HMS Catherwood's directors. Courtesy B Boyle. UFTM L3782/4

From the mid-1920s until the formation of the NIRTB in 1935 several independent operators provided bus services in the Ballymena district. Some worked in the Braid Valley and others provided services to Dunloy, Randalstown and Toome. One of the latter was Frederick Howe of Ballymena who began to run a bus between Ballymena, Ahoghill and Toome about 1926. At first his only opposition came from Robert Agnew of Portglenone who, at the time was running a bus between Portglenone and Ballymena which went over the same route as Howe's bus between Ahoghill and Ballymena. On 26 September 1928 a more serious rival appeared on the same road, – W Kerr of Toome who started to run buses between Toome, Randalstown and Ballymena. Initially his buses went via Slatt and Whiteside Corner to avoid going over exactly the same as Howe; nevertheless, the latter realised that a competitor for the Ballymena-Randalstown traffic had arrived and immediately cut his fares, a challenge to which Kerr replied on 10 December by re-routing two of his buses via Ahoghill. After two months Howe withdrew and devoted his energies on the service between Ballymena and Dunloy which he had opened in the previous year. Kerr, on the other hand, continued to develop his services, so that, in the mid-1930s, his buses were providing four double workings between Ballymena and Randalstown, three between Ballymena and Toomebridge, three between Ballymena and New Ferry, as well as Sunday services which, in the words of a police report, were 'wholly for the purpose of conveying people to divine service at Portglenone and Moneydig', the latter place being near Toomebridge. At the 1935 take over, Kerr owned five Dennis buses, four of which were 20-seaters.

On the road to Dunloy, Howe had to face competition from buses of the Bann Motor Service Company Ltd, which ran between Ballymena and Kilrea and used the same road as far as Cullybackey, a route on which Bann MS sometimes provided five double workings compared with the four worked by Howe's buses. On Saturdays, however, Howe provided a half-hourly service between Ballymena and Cullybackey. The introduction of this caused considerable resentment among the hackney car owners in the district who, in February 1930, employed a solicitor to draw up a petition which was sent to the Minister of Home Affairs at Stormont stating that the intensity of the new service was depriving them of their livelihoods. Before becoming an omnibus proprietor, Howe had owned a wholesale confectionery and tobacco business in Ballymena, and during his time in buses had traded initially as the Dunloy Motor Service and then as the Maine Auto Service, whereas Kerr had always run his buses as the Kerr Bus Service. On 3 December 1935 Howe transferred his three buses (2 Bedford; 1 Dodge) to the NIRTB. In addition to the services already mentioned, there was also a twice-daily local working between Rasharkin and the railway station at Cullybackey. In 1927 this was provided by W Hay but, shortly afterwards the maintenance of the service passed to R C Smyth.[2]

Early in 1927 Thomas Montgomery of Upper Buckna and James Jamieson of Broughshane started to run buses in the Braid Valley. Both used the main road from Ballymena to Broughshane where Montgomery's buses turned off southwards to Lisnamurrican and then proceeded in an easterly direction over secondary roads to Buckna and Carnalbana, whereas those of Jamieson continued along the Carnlough Road to The Sheddings, some eight miles from Broughshane. In addition to providing two double workings daily between Buckna and Ballymena, Montgomery also ran a Market Bus between Buckna and Larne. This left the former at 0845 hrs on Wednesday mornings and was due in Larne about an hour and a half later, his passengers being charged 1s 6d for their 18-mile journey (2s 6d return). Jamieson usually provided four double workings between Ballymena and The Sheddings and, on market days, he usually ran one or two licenced hackney cars with his buses so that no prospective passengers would be left behind. Both proprietors understood the needs of the Braid people and provided reliable and adequate services and, during the summer, each of them ran special trips from Ballymena and Lisnamurrican to the seaside at Cushendall and Carnlough for which their patrons were charged a return fare of 2s 6d. In 1935 Montgomery owned two 20-seater buses (Bedford; Dennis) and Jamieson possessed two 20-seater Commers. In 1928 James Ramsey of Broughshane began to run a 20-seater Bedford between Ballymena and Broughshane using the back road via Raceview, his passengers being charged a single fare of 4d, with no reduction for return tickets!

County Armagh

Six omnibus proprietors in Armagh never joined either the BOC or the GNR. Three of them had gone out of business before the formation of the NIRTB and the remainder survived to join the new organisation in 1935.

The longest-established of these was Joseph McCabe of Waringstown who had been already over 40 years in the hackney car business when he formed the Favourite Bus Service in the mid-1920s. His buses ran between Lurgan, Banbridge, Donacloney and Portadown, his principal service was that between Lurgan and Donacloney on which 14 double workings were provided on weekdays with an additional 10 runs on Saturdays. In September 1929 he came to an agreement with the BOC, whereby he would give up his Lurgan-Portadown and Lurgan-Banbridge services whilst the Belfast company would cease workings between Lurgan and Dromore via Donacloney. At the formation of the NIRTB, his five buses (4 Dennis; 1 Commer) were taken over by the new authority.

Joseph Poots of Dromore, who was one of the proprietors of the Frontier Bus Service which ran

105. Poots Bedford WLB bus Reg IB 5496. Joseph Poots buses were stabled in Church Place, Lurgan where CW Drysdale carried on a garage business. Bookings for Wednesday and weekend mystery tours could be made at McNabb's the chemists. Date, c.1933. UFTM L1527/11

between Newry and Belfast, also owned the Glider buses which started a service between Lurgan and Portadown via Bleary and Knocknamuckly in the mid-1920s. In 1932 he purchased, at a cost of £550, the two 14-seater buses (Chevrolet; Morris) which Herbert Gray of Portadown had been running on a rival service over the same route since 1928. A year before this Gray had started his career as a bus operator by running a service between Armagh, Markethill and Whitecross but, after a few months, he changed his route to one between Portadown and Lurgan via Bleary. He usually provided four double workings and advertised his service as the Citizen Bus Service. In 1930 he got into serious trouble with the Ministry of Home Affairs for increasing his fares without permission. This so incensed him that he withdrew his buses for a few weeks early in 1931 and, a year later, sold them to Poots. The latter also had his troubles for he was continually being plagued by illegal competition from hackney carriage proprietors and private car owners who, on busy days, poached his traffic by running their cars a short distance in front of his buses, which were restricted by having to keep to a published timetable. In addition, his application to the ministry for permission to run a town service in Lurgan was refused as there were already five operators working in the area, namely BOC to Belfast, Dromore and Portadown; the GNR to Belfast direct and via Aghalee; McCabe to Donacloney; McLearnon to Bannfoot and Gawley's Gate; and Poots, himself, to Portadown, a route in which his Glider Buses usually provided eight double workings daily with additional workings on Thursdays and Saturdays and a very limited service on Sundays. When his service was taken over by the NIRTB, Poots owned four buses (2 Bedford; 1 Dennis; 1 Leyland).

Three buses, all owned by different proprietors, provided services between Lurgan and the shores of Lough Neagh. The first was John McLearnon of Lurgan who acquired a bus in 1928 with which he provided a local service between Lurgan and Aghagallon, Derrytrasna and Gawley's Gate. Shortly afterwards, Alexander Wallace of Lurgan, began to run a twice-weekly bus between Lurgan and Portadown via Bannfoot which competed with McLearnon's Derrytrasna service between Derryadd and Lurgan. After a few months Wallace withdrew, and his bus was acquired by Thomas Castles of Derryadd who, at the time, was running a bi-weekly service with a 14-seater Morris between Lurgan and Bannfoot. In 1930 he was bought out by McLearnon for £250, who continued to work in this part of Armagh under the name of the Lagan Queen Bus Service, until the acquisition of his two 14-seater Reos by the NIRTB.

In July 1920 the Newtownhamilton garage owners John and Robert John Steen began to provide the first regular motor bus service to Newry. Their buses carried the name *The Reliance* and for five years the Steens were the only operators to run buses in south Armagh. In the mid-1920s they were joined by John McCourt who began a service between Crossmaglen and Newry which he transferred to the BOC in March 1928. Immediately after this the Steens put on a rival bus to Crossmaglen, but withdrew it after a few months and in its place extended four of its Newry-Newtownhamilton workings to Cullyhanna. But the roads to Cullyhanna were so narrow, and in such bad condition, and patronage was so poor, that after a short time the workings on this route were reduced to one per day. In 1929 the Steens increased their route mileage by extending some of their Newry-Newtownhamilton runs to Armagh and, at about the same time, followed the example of many other operators by running Sunday buses to the seaside, in their case it was to Warrenpoint. At the take over in 1935 the Steens were operating four small buses (2 Chevrolet; 2 Bedford).

County Down

Previous to the setting up of the NIRTB, the largest bus owners in County Down were the BOC and GNR, with the latter being more prominent in the west of the county. Nevertheless, about 20 other omnibus proprietors continued as independent operators until the autumn of 1935. Ten of these were in north Down, six in south Down and the remainder within a triangle bounded by Belfast, Banbridge and Lurgan.

North Down

At one time or another, numerous omnibus proprietors were involved in operating bus services in north Down. Some of these went out of business, others had joined the BOC and ten continued to run buses until the NIRTB take over. Three of the last mentioned group – James McCartney, the Imperial Bus Service, and the Kane Brothers of Millisle – competed with the BOC on the busy Belfast-Newtownards Road where, at times, the fares for the ten-mile journey would be reduced to 6d single, 9d return. The others ran local services in an area bounded by Bangor, Newtownards and Ballywalter.

On 4 February 1924 the Pioneer Motor Service, which was owned by James McCartney

106. McCartney's Garner PA bus Reg IJ 8993. The 20-seater bus was supplied new in 1928. The spare tyre is completely bald. R Ludgate Collection. UFTM L3773/2

107. McCartney's Pickie Commer Centaur bus Reg BZ 2457. This 20-seater vehicle was new in 1934, taken over by the NIRTB in 1935 and finally withdrawn in 1944. Courtesy B Boyle. UFTM L3782/3

of Newtownards, began to run buses to Belfast.[3] Initially five double workings were provided and his buses were timed to do the journey in 45 minutes; by 1928 the frequency had been increased to a minimum of 12 double workings with some additional runs on Saturdays. He was a man of many interests; he owned a hotel at Pickie in Bangor and ran the Pickie bus tours from the same town. These were usually worked by his Pioneer buses, with the addition of a board labelled 'Pickie Tours.' In 1935 he owned nine buses (2 Bedford; 1 Commer; 2 Dennis 1 Leyland; 3 Garner) all of which were painted blue. Three years before this, he came to an agreement with Samuel Davidson of Comber to take over Davidson's service, but the sale (see page 30), was forbidden by the government which ruled that as Davidson was mainly concerned in running buses between Comber and Belfast, the BOC should be offered first refusal of his business. The BOC accepted the offer and in July 1932 his four buses (2 Leyland; 2 Lancia) were acquired by the Belfast company. In September 1925, Davidson had begun to run buses between Comber and Belfast, and by 1930 they were providing an hourly service over this route. He also worked rural services from Comber to Ballyhorn and Ballymacashan and, during the summer, ran a Sunday afternoon bus from Comber to Bangor which was timed to give its patrons a whole afternoon at the seaside.

In November 1925, William Crawford of Belfast began to run the Imperial buses between Millisle, Donaghadee, Newtownards and Belfast and, by 1927, was providing six round trips daily over this route, the time for the 18 miles from Donaghadee to Belfast being 55 minutes; by 1928 the frequency had been increased to fifteen. In July of the same year Crawford entered the Belfast Bus War by running buses between Balmoral and Strandtown.[4] This had to stop later in the year when new regulations restored to the city its monopoly for the provision of public transport within its boundaries. As a result, the ten Dennis buses which the Imperial BS had been using on its city service, were sold to the Corporation. In April 1929 Crawford purchased the three small Chevrolet buses which Mrs Anna Stewart of Donaghadee had been running between Bangor and Donaghadee since 1926, and then continued to operate them on the same route until the end of the season. He then sold them to J H O'Neill of Bangor and, six months later Crawford sold the Imperial Omnibus Service to S H Weir and A S Baird of Belfast, eight buses (6 AEC; 1 ADC; 1 Dennis) changing hands in the transaction. Its new owners, who had at one time been the proprietors of the International and the Woodburn Bus Services, were also the Commer agents for Northern Ireland and gradually re-equipped the

108. Imperial Buse Service Commer NF6 bus reg BZ 181 at Sand Quay, Belfast. The vehicle was new in 1930 and was taken over by the NIRTB on 1 Nov 1935. Courtesy B Boyle. UFTM L3782/2.

109. Ex Imperial bus Reg BZ 181 now in NIRTB livery. The sign on the rear of the vehicle reads, 'Please sound horn as we wish to extend the courtesy of the road'. This bus was withdrawn in 1937. Photographer A Campbell. UFTM L3778/5

Imperial fleet with ten Commer buses which, along with a 32-seater Gilford, passed to the NIRTB in 1935. Before the Weir and Baird take-over, the Imperial buses were advertised as the 'yellow buses with black roofs' but their new owners changed their livery to yellow and brown.

The Imperial buses did not enjoy a long monopoly on the Millisle road for, on 27 March 1926, the Kane brothers of Millisle began a competitive service to Belfast via Killaughey, Loughries and Newtownards. Within a short time their maroon and cream Gilford buses, which all carried the name *Millisle Queen*, where running eight round trips to the city and were continuing to provide this type of service when their four buses (1 Graham-Dodge; 3 Gilford) were acquired by the NIRTB.

Four local operators also ran buses in Donaghadee and the Lower Ards. The first of these to go on the road was Robert McGivern of Carrowdore, who began to run a horse car between Carrowdore and Newtownards in 1905. A small Ford bus obtained in 1919 was replaced in 1929 with a 14-seater Chevrolet, which continued to run three round trips daily to Newtownards until the NIRTB take-over in 1935. Despite numerous requests, the government never permitted him to work to Belfast but he was allowed to run buses from Carrowdore to Ballywalter and Millisle during the summer. The next local operator was James Shilliday of Bangor who began to run his *Britannia* charabanc between Bangor and Donaghadee in 1913; six years later he obtained two new solid-tyred charabancs which he named *Bluebird* and *Seabird*. At the outbreak of the 1914-18 War he purchased a Commer chassis, on which he mounted a truck body, and used the vehicle to take flax and other materials to local mills. During holiday periods he replaced the truck body with one fitted with seats and used the vehicle as a charabanc.[5] It was probable that this was the motor which was commandeered by the Royal Irish Constabulary to take some police to Galway during the week of the 1916 Easter Rising, the vehicle being driven there and back by James Shilliday, himself. In the early 1920s Shilliday began to run buses between Donaghadee and Belfast and, at about the same time, W Rankine joined him as a partner. The union, however, was never particularly satisfactory and broke up in 1926 when their bus fleet (1 Commer; 1AEC; 2 Leyland) was sold to Moore Bros of Donaghadee.[6] After this, Shilliday reverted to his original business of road freight haulage. The third omnibus proprietor was Robert Lawther of Ballywalter who, in the mid-1920s, owned a 20-seater blue and cream Reo which usually worked one round trip each weekday between Ballywalter and Belfast via Carrowdore, as well as providing several shuttle runs between Ballywalter, Carrowdore and Newtownards where connections were made with McCartney's buses for Belfast. Indeed, the latter's printed timetables always included a list of the arrival and departure times of the Lawther buses in Newtownards. In February 1929 Robert handed over the working of the service to his brother James, who continued to operate it until the NIRTB took over its working together with the three buses (1 Commer; 2 Reo) and the private-hire business which the two brothers also ran. The fourth operator was T V Weir of Newtownards who, in the 1930s, ran buses between Newtownards and Belfast via Craigantlet. Finally, a certain John Bennett was reputed to have run a bus in the Donaghadee area in the spring of 1929. Little is known about this service other than a report to the Ministry of Home Affairs which states that ministry investigators could trace neither Mr Bennett nor his bus!

South Down

Seven of the local bus owners serving the south Down area retained their independence until being absorbed into the NIRTB in 1935.

One of these is the oldest undertaking associated with road transport in the province. As far back as Napoleanic times, the McAnulty Family has owned a posting establishment in Warrenpoint. In 1915 it acquired its first motor, a yellow Caledon charabanc, which was registered in the name of Hugh McAnulty. This was in the year when the horse-operated tramway between

110. Yellow Line Motor Service Caledon charabanc which Hugh McAnulty began operating in 1915, the same year as the Warrenpoint and Rostrevor Tramway closed. The McAnulty family are still bus operators today. Courtesy: W Montgomery. UFTM L1528/6

Warrenpoint and Rostrevor closed down, after which the McAnulty charabanc began to meet many of the trains at Warrenpoint station. By 1928 the McAnulty buses, which were advertised as the Yellow Line Motor Service were providing three double workings between Warrenpoint and Kilkeel with an additional eight round trips between Warrenpoint and Rostrevor Quay. Members of the McAnulty Family often drove buses themselves, especially when they were hired to take teams to football matches; indeed, it is claimed that the drivers often substituted with distinction[7] when their 'customers' were short of players! When the transport section of their business was acquired by the NIRTB, five buses (1 Albion; 1 Chevrolet; 2 Dennis; 1 Reo) were involved in the transaction.

In 1927 Bernard Cregan and Michael McNally, both of whom came from Newry, began to run rival buses between Newry and Dromintee and, shortly afterwards, McNally also started to operate a 14-seater bus between Newry and Hagan's Bridge via Killeen Chapel. In October they came to an understanding whereby each would work six services out of Newry on weekdays. Cregan's bus would follow the main road to Forkhill and McNally's would go to Dromintee via Ballinless and Finnegan's Cross; this meant that both owners would have to use the same road between Newry and Meigh. Cregan withdrew his bus in 1930, after which the Forkhill service was provided by McNally, who continued to work in this part of south Armagh until his three small buses (1 Graham-Dodge; 2 Dennis) were taken over by the NIRTB.

Buses first arrived in Rathfriland in 1923 when D A Crory began a service to Belfast which was taken over by the BOC four years later. However, the BOC seems to have made little serious effort to extend its influence in the Rathfriland neighbourhood, which continued to be well-served by a network of rural buses owned by local operators. Many of these had already acquired considerable experience in horse-drawn public transport before changing to motor buses. One of these, W E Martin, had driven a horse-drawn car between Rathfriland and the railway station at Ballyroney until he acquired a motor bus of his own on 14 October 1926. This he ran over the same road and charged his passengers the same sixpenny fare as in his horse-drawn days but now the three-mile journey took only a quarter of an hour. At about the same time he opened a new twice-daily service between Rathfriland and Dechomet. By 1905, the Downey family of Rathfriland had already become well established on the road to Newry via Hilltown, and about 20 years later they made the change from horse-drawn long cars to buses. These were painted green with a white band and were registered in the name of Charles Downey.[8] They usually provided five double workings with additional services on Thursdays and Saturdays. During the summer months they also ran a bus from Rathfriland to Warrenpoint via Kilcoo and Hilltown, a trip which took about 1hr 45min and on which the return fare cost 2s 6d. In 1930 the Downeys extended their coverage by opening a thrice-daily service between Newry and Glascar, which they continued to work until the end of 1935, when the NIRTB purchased their five 20-seater buses (1 Bedford; 2 Commer; 2 Reo).

In the 1930s the Downeys had to face very serious competition from R Stevenson & Son who owned an engineering business in Rathfriland which had, at one time, specialised in the repair of agricultural machinery and had become involved with motor cars shortly after these arrived in the district.[9] In 1919 they obtained the first motor charabanc to run in this part of County Down and, shortly afterwards, began a regular bus ser-

111. Chevrolet and Bedford buses belonging to R Stevenson of Rathfriland. The second bus from the right is a 14 seater Chevrolet, supplied new in 1928 to R Revels. Date, c.1935. UFTM L3728/2

vice between Rathfriland and Castlewellan on which some of the workings were extended to Newcastle during holiday periods. In November 1930 they obtained an entry into the Rathfriland-Newry passenger trade by purchasing the 14-seater Reo which Ralph Revels was then operating on the route. Revels had acquired the bus about a year previously from his brother-in-law, Robert J Irwin who was a joint-owner of the Irwin buses, which ran between Lurgan and Belfast. He is also credited with the running of the first bus between Rathfriland and Newry, which is claimed to have taken place in 1925. A few months later he commenced a thrice-daily service between Banbridge, Newry and Warrenpoint with buses which had names ending in the word star, eg *Ulster Star*. In 1929 he withdrew from providing local road transport in this part of County Down and disposed of his three 14-seater buses, with the Chevrolet going to Revels, the Reo to the Stevensons and the third to an anonymous buyer. Immediately after this acquisition, the Stevensons revised their Rathfriland-Castlewellan timetable to synchronise with that of their Rathfriland-Newry buses, thereby providing several through workings each day between Castlewellan and Newry. They also took over the workings of Revel's shuttle service which ran between Newry and Camlough on Camlough fair days, a route on which the Downeys also provided a similar fair day service. The rivalry between these two operators was not only economic but, on occasions, became somewhat political when 'neither political party would travel in the other party's bus.' In 1935 the Stevensons possessed six buses (2 Bedford; 2 Chevrolets; 1 Guy; 1 Lancia).

In the 1880s William Finlay of Castlewellan began to carry passengers and mail in a horse-drawn car between Castlewellan and Newcastle. Nearly 50 years later he obtained his first motor bus and, in the summer of 1930 was providing eight double workings over the same road. Another operator in this area was Michael Clarke of Leitrim who, in the early 1930s, began to run a local service between Hilltown and Bryansford via Foffany as well as a Thursday-only market service from Castlewellan to Ballynahinch. He also worked Monday-only services between Castlewellan and the Square, which is near Kilcoo, and from Castlewellan to Leitrim. In 1935 Finlay's 20-seater Guy and Clarke's 20-seater Garner were acquired by the NIRTB.

North West Down

In the decade before the formation of the NIRTB the area within a triangle bounded by Belfast, Banbridge and Lurgan was served by a host of bus operators who owned one or two buses which often changed ownership as their proprietors entered, or retired from, the road transport business. Only three were still in operation at the NIRTB take-over.

The most remunerative trade for small operators in this area was that between the city and the Purdysburn Hospital complex, where competition was so intense that, in March 1930, four of the operators engaged in this service agreed to implement a timetable which had been drawn up for them by the police, whereby each of them would get an equitable share of the market. The four were John Wilson, David Lawther, William Scott and McCreight & Ross. The first mentioned ran his buses from Agnes Street in Belfast and the other three from Ormeau Avenue; all charged the same fares (6d single, 9d return) and they ran at times to suit visiting hours in the hospitals. Wilson, who lived on the Shankill Road, was mainly interested in private-hire work and retained his independence until his bus, a Gilford 28-seater, was taken over by the NIRTB. David Lawther, who had served in a Royal Navy armoured car squadron in the Caucasus during the 1914-18 War, had been running buses between Drumbeg and Belfast via Ballylesson since 1925. In 1928, he was providing eleven double workings over this route as well as running to and from the hospitals on visiting days. Over the next seven years he built up his business so that, when he was taken over by the NIRTB he was the owner of eight buses (1 Albion; 1 Chevrolet; 3 Commer; 1 Dennis; 1 Leyland; 1 Reo). The third Drumbo operator was William

112. Drumbo Queen Morris bus operated by John Burton of Belfast. This photograph was taken outside Harkness' Coach Factory, Dover Street, Belfast who built the body. John Burton eventually became a driving instructor with BCT. Date, 1926. UFTM L477/6

Scott, who had been providing a minimum service of five round workings between Belfast and Leveroge since 1927, but he went out of business in 1930 and sold his 20-seater Chevrolet to Sydney Harrison who, within a few months disposed of it to David Lawther. At about the same time Scott's other two buses (Garner; Reo) were acquired by the much-experienced Antrim bus owner, Joseph McNeilly, who now purchased the Purdysburn MS from McCreight & Ross and continued to operate it until the NIRTB took over his four buses (2 Dennis; 2 Leyland). The Purdysburn MS[10] had been formed early in 1927 and, in addition to the hospital service, also ran between Belfast and Ballycowan, a route on which some of the buses were routed via Milltown and the others via Newtownbreda. The former went by the Malone Road and, like the buses belonging to William Scott, were permitted by Belfast Corporation to take up, and set down, local passengers within the city boundary, the only stipulation being that such people had to pay a minimum fare of 4d irrespective of how far they were travelling within the city limits.

In January 1932 William Nevin of Belfast paid £563 for the two 20-seater Reos with which William Martin of Lisburn had been maintaining a service between Belfast and Purdysburn since the late 1920s. After the purchase he continued to operate the same service until the NIRTB takeover in 1935. Another Purdysburn operator who, like Martin, was not a party to the 1930 agreement, was John Burton of Belfast who ran the Drumbo Queen Bus Service. When the Belfast Bus War began in June 1928 he transferred two of his buses to run in the city and, when it ended, one of the vehicles was purchased by the corporation. After this, Burton continued to operate in the Drumbo area and two years later acquired the 20-seater Dennis which W Knutt had also been running between Belfast and Drumbo. At about the same time he applied for permission to open a new service which was to run from Belfast to Conlig via Craigantlet. Permission was refused and late in 1932 Burton left the business and sold his service to W Dow, who had at one time run the Diamond Bus between Crumlin and Belfast.

A somewhat unsuccessful operator was E Gregory of Hillsborough who, in 1927, acquired a 24-seater Gilford safety coach which he used somewhat intermittently on the road between Lisburn and Belfast. He also provided a service from Lisburn to the hospitals at Purdysburn on visiting days and a church run to take worshippers from Hilden to Lisburn on Sunday mornings. Like many other small operators, he became involved in the 1928 Belfast Bus War and, when this ended his bus was taken over by the corporation and he retired from the road passenger business.

County Fermanagh

None of the four local bus proprietors living in Fermanagh joined the NIRTB in 1935. However, two of them had become members before the outbreak of the 1939–45 War; a third, who ran some cross-border services, retained his independence until 1957 when he joined the Ulster Transport Authority, which had taken over from the NIRTB in 1948. The fourth had been absorbed by another Fermanagh bus operator in 1933.

On 10 February 1926 Hezekiah Appleby chartered a bus to take some traders from Belcoo to the fair at Enniskillen. At about the same time he formed the Central Omnibus Company and, shortly afterwards, his buses were providing two double workings between Enniskillen and Sligo, the time allowed for their 42-mile journey being 2hr 30min for which their passengers were charged fares of 5s single and 7s 6d return. In 1929 he extended his activities by providing a summer service of two double workings between Enniskillen and Bundoran via Belcoo and Lough Melvin, two hours being required for the 38 miles. Shortly after the formation of the NIRTB he was refused permission to work north of the border, and the goodwill of his services in Northern Ireland, together with two of his 20-seater buses (Bedford; Gilford), were compulsorily acquired by the new organisation on 3 December 1937. Appleby continued to run buses between Blacklion (a village in the Free State adjacent to the Fermanagh border town of Belcoo) and Sligo until he sold this part of his undertaking to the Sligo, Leitrim & Northern Counties Railway,[11] the two buses concerned being transferred on 2 April 1945.

The first bus to run to Derrygonnelly was owned by Captain S B Merrilies and was driven by his son-in-law, William Clarke. In due course, Clarke took over from his father-in-law and by mid-1927 his two 14-seater buses were providing regular services between Enniskillen and Derrylin and from Enniskillen to Derrygonnelly, two double workings being provided on each route. Shortly afterwards he extended his services to include Fivemiletown and Rosslea and began to carry pilgrims to and from Lough Derg, near Pettigo. Early in 1930 he requested the Northern Ireland government for permission to work between Enniskillen and Carrick-on-Shannon on a service which had been started by W E White in the late 1920s (see page 65). When this was refused, he circumvented the veto by starting a short lived, thrice weekly, service between Carrick and Blacklion, from which place his Enniskillen passengers were taken in a motor car for a journey of a few hundred yards to the railway station in Belcoo, which was on the northern side of the border. In 1933 Clarke took over the two small buses (Chevrolet; Graham-Dodge) with which E W McCreery had been operating the Hard Rocks Motor Service at Lisbellaw; these ran between Enniskillen and Tempo, some of the buses being routed via Garvary and the others via Lisbellaw. In the early 1930s McCreery failed to get permission to extend his workings from Tempo to Fintona on the grounds that the road between Fivemiletown and Fintona, over which it was intended his buses should travel, was not suitable for heavy vehicles. On the other hand he was permitted to run buses to Bundoran during the summer holidays. Clarke continued to operate the services provided by McCreery and also commenced a new weekday working from Enniskillen to Belleek via the northern shore of Lough Erne. In 1936 he owned four 20-seater buses (1 Dennis; 2 Guy; 1 Manchester) which were painted blue and advertised as Clarke's Blue Bus Services. Shortly after its acquisition in 1936 by the NIRTB, the Manchester was taken out of service, but the other three remained in use until the 1939-45 War; however, by this time Clarke had received a cheque for £5050 from their new owners.

The Erne Bus Service was started by M Cassidy on 8 March 1929 and by the mid-1930s his brown and cream 20-seaters were working between Enniskillen and Clones (five double workings), along the southern shore of Lough Erne to Belleek and Bundoran and also to Cavan and to Cootehill via Clones. At this time he owned five buses (1 Chevrolet; 3 Commer; 1 Graham Dodge) and had already established his company's practice of always starting his buses three minutes late to facilitate the habitually unpunctual.[12] The Erne BS retained its independence mainly because of its trans-border services, which it continued to provide until its merger in 1957 with the Devenish Carriage and Wagon Company, a subsidiary of the UTA. However, its eight buses (7 Leyland; 1 Dodge), three of which were of pre-1933 vintage, continued to trade under their old name.

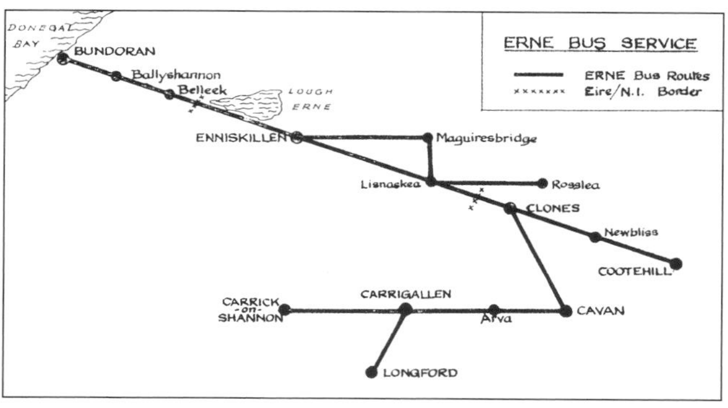

113. Route Map of Erne Bus Service.

County Londonderry

Bus services in Ulster usually originated in villages or small towns, to facilitate travel to larger market towns. In Co Londonderry it was different: here it was city businessmen in Derry who decided to improve communications with neighbouring villages. Furthermore, due to the energetic buy-up policy adopted by HMS Catherwood and the NCC, by the time of the NIRTB takeover, there was only one independent bus operator left in the county.

The earliest omnibus service in the county was that between Derry and Greencastle, County Donegal, which was started by the three Roberts brothers, the owners of the City of Derry Garage. Their first bus[13] was scheduled to leave Derry at 0600 hrs on Saturday, 1 June 1912. About a quarter of an hour before this, it commenced a 'milk run' in which it collected travellers from each of the four leading hotels in the city. The bus (32-seater Lacre charabanc) was timed to cover the 20 miles (3 miles of which were in Londonderry County) between Derry and Greencastle in 1hr 40 min, for which its passengers were charged 2s single, 3s 6d return. Initially two double workings were made on weekdays but this had been increased to six by 1927 and the time of the journey reduced to 1hr 20 min.

Two months after the opening of the Greencastle service, the Roberts Bros began a daily working between Derry and Feeny, a working which was subsequently extended to Dungiven (21 miles from Derry) and the number of workings increased to two. On 25 July 1929, buses of the Belfast-owned Independent BS began to run between Belfast and Dungiven. Shortly afterwards, the schedules of both operators were adjusted to enable their buses to connect at Dungiven, thereby enabling passengers to travel by bus between Belfast and Derry by making one change of bus en route. However, the Stormont government forbade either operator to run through buses between Belfast and Derry and often issued warnings to the Independent BS that their buses travelling to Dungiven must display Dungiven, and not Derry, on their destination blinds.

On 1 June 1927, Roberts Bros commenced a twice daily service between Derry and Ballybofey which was allowed 1hr 40min for the 25 miles (four miles of which were in County Londonderry).[14] By 1929 this frequency had been increased to six but, by this time, the brothers sensed that the ambition of Catherwood and the NCC was to buy out every independent bus operator in the county. The Roberts' response was to get out of the road passenger business as quickly as possible and, within the next year, had disposed of fourteen of their buses and charabancs with six going to the GNR (3 Dennis; 2 Chevrolet; 1 Gilford); four to the NCC (2 Chevrolet; 2 Dennis); four to James Winter's County Donegal Motor Service (3 Chevrolet; 1 Reo). Thereafter, Roberts Bros confined their activities to running their garage and providing charabancs and buses for private-hire.

On 25 April 1925 WHC Galt of Coleraine opened a service between Coleraine and Ballymena via Ballymoney and Kilrea[15] but closed it down later in the same year when he began to run between Coleraine and Garvagh instead. It seems he possessed only one bus and, early in 1927, he traded it in part exchange for a new 26-seater Reo. The replacement was late in arriving, so his service was temporarily closed down. He became desperate in trying to get a replacement so, when a new 26-seater Reo arrived in Coleraine for David Lyttle of Castlerock, he borrowed it when it was left unattended in The Diamond. He attempted to justify his action by claiming the bus was his, but had been wrongly allocated by the local Reo distributors, an excuse which did not prevent him from appearing at Coleraine Petty Sessions in March of that year;[16] after this he retired from being a purveyor of public transport. David Lyttle ran a somewhat intermittent service[17] from Coleraine to Castlerock in 1927.

By the time of the NIRTB take-over in 1935, Catherwood and the NCC had just failed by one to get possession of all the privately owned bus services in the county. The one that got away was Henry's Motor Service, which was the direct descendant of the posting business established by S R Henry in 1890. In its early days the company ran jaunting cars and horse-drawn brakes, and in 1914 acquired its first motor car. In 1920 it obtained a 14-seater charabanc[18] and in 1922 started a charabanc service along the coast road between Portstewart and Portrush. This prospered and by 1930 a half-hourly service was being provided during July and August when an average of a thousand passengers used it each day; the fares charged being 2d single and 3d return. The company also ran an intensive service between Portstewart town centre and the Strand and, on the closure of the Portstewart Tramway in 1926, it began to provide a subsidised bus service between the town and its railway station at Culmore. When the NCC withdrew this subsidy in 1932, the service ceased to be financially viable and the bus was withdrawn. The Henry charabancs also ran short day tours to Glenarriff and other places of interest and provided coaches on long-term hire to tour operators such as the Holiday Fellowship. At the take-over by the NIRTB, Henry was the owner of nine buses (6 Dennis; 3 Leyland) which had red bodies, green waistbands, black roofs and their wheels were yellow.

114. Henry's Coast Tours bus at Portstewart c1930. The conductor is cranking the handle to start the engine. UFTM L456/1

115. Henry's Coast Tours Thornycroft charabanc Reg XD 8114 photographed at Portstewart. This vehicle was first registered on 9 May 1921 to the Samuelson Transport Co Ltd of 28 Denmount Street, London and was subsequently registered to SS Henry on 4 May 1923 and was last licenced in 1932. Ulster Museum Welch collection. WO7/52/2

County Tyrone

At the time of the NIRTB take-over there were four bus owners running services in Tyrone, one of whom (GNR) also ran into Derry city. The principal operator was the GNR, which provided services between the larger towns in the county; W E Hobson operated a fleet of 15 buses in the Dungannon-Cookstown area; and the other two, Mrs Charlton and W A Simpson, were both based in Omagh.

In 1935 public transport in the Dungannon area was being provided by the GNR and the Hobson Motor Service. The former ran to Belfast, Monaghan and Omagh, and the latter to Armagh, Cookstown, Omagh and Portadown, its busiest route being that to Cookstown and Coalisland. It was owned by W E Hobson of Dungannon, who began a service between Dungannon and Cookstown in August 1927, a route on which N W Brodie (who managed the Pilot BS of Portadown) had been active since August 1925, trading under the name of the Reliable AS (see page 27). Brodie ran four Vulcan buses which he had obtained from W H Reay, the Vulcan agent in Belfast. Three years later they were seized, as Brodie was £600 in arrears with his hire purchase payments to Reay and also owed £100 to W Davidson of Coalisland for petrol. On getting repossession of his buses, Reay changed the name of the company from the Reliable Auto Service to the Regent Bus Service and transferred his buses to Belfast to participate in the Belfast Bus War. When this ended, he brought them back to run on their old route between Dungannon and Coalisland. During their absence in Belfast, Hobson had restored the single fare for the 4-mile journey between Dungannon and Coalisland to 5d, the fare having been reduced to 2d when the Brodie-Hobson competition was at its height. In January 1929 Hobson acquired the Regent BS, but this did not end his troubles since Davidson, who owned a garage in Coalisland and had managed the Regent BS for Reay, started his own bus service between Coalisland and Dungannon which he advertised as the 'Regent Bus Service', thereby providing the choice between two services each trading under the same name! This option ended when Hobson acquired the second Regent Bus Service in 1931.

Hobson made a somewhat better purchase in March 1930 when he spent £2000 acquiring three buses (1 Dennis; 1 Reo; 1 Thornycroft) which John McGirr of Dungannon had been running between Dungannon and Omagh via Pomeroy; Dungannon and Portadown via The Moy; and on a short-lived service between Dungannon and Armagh during the winter of 1927/28. Hobson, himself, expanded his service to Armagh in 1928, and by 1933 was providing five double workings over the route, his buses being timed to cover the 13 miles in 45 minutes. In the early 1930s one of the buses on this route was scheduled to leave Armagh just after the close of the cinema in that city, but when Dungannon got a picture house of its own in 1933, patronage of this late working got so poor that it was withdrawn in the late summer of that year.

By 1935 Hobson had become one of the largest omnibus proprietors outside Belfast. On weekdays his buses provided services on 20 routes. The busiest was that between Dungannon and

116. Hobson's Leyland bus fitted with Leyland body. By 1935 Hobson was one of the largest rural operators in Ulster. Courtesy B Boyle. UFTM L1529/7

Cookstown on which there were 8 double workings, three of which continued to the Battery on the shore of Lough Neagh. Other routes connected Dungannon with Omagh, via Pomeroy, as well as to Armagh and Portadown; the latter were routes via The Moy or via Loughgall. He also ran market day services to Benburb, Eglish and other small towns in the vicinity of Dungannon and Armagh, and also carried on quite a busy private-hire business. His published timetable had, by then, become a 24-page booklet setting out not only his bus times but also the conditions under which passengers were carried, advertisements from local traders and full details as to how bicycles were to be carried on his buses. This stated that bicycles 'will only be carried upon the roofs of buses upon which provision for luggage has been made and under no circumstances will they be carried inside the bus. A charge of half the ordinary fare will be made for each bicycle carried.

Unfortunately Hobson, who relied on the very competent Mrs Hobson for the day-to-day running of his business, was always having trouble with Davidson, whom he never forgave for re-establishing the Regent BS, and also with James Winter, the local GNR road service manager. He accused the two of them of enticing his better employees into their organisations, of running non-scheduled buses over authorised and unauthorised routes and of fare-cutting. They reciprocated by accusing him of the same

117. Simpson's Fleetwing buses operated between Omagh-Enniskillen and Omagh-Castlederg. All Simpson's bus fleet had registration numbers which ended in 7. Courtesy R L Morrison. UFTM L3716/2

misdemeanours! The situation was eased a little when Winter negotiated the purchase of the Regent BS on behalf of the GNR, but since he had failed to keep his employers informed of what he had done he was unable to finalise the transaction. This lapse enabled Hobson himself to acquire the Regent BS in June 1931, but by this time Winter had left the railway's employment. Hobson's troubles finally ended in November 1935 when the NIRTB acquired his 14 buses, eleven of which were Leylands.

The two services based in Omagh were operated by William A Simpson and Mrs Margaret Charlton. The former owned the Fleetwing Bus Service which began to run between Omagh and Enniskillen in November 1927. A year later Simpson re-opened the service between Omagh and Castlederg via Drumquin which traversed a thinly-populated area over which Donaghy had made an unsuccessful attempt to run buses in 1926 (see page 61). Simpson not only re-opened the service on a bi-weekly basis with buses making two double workings on Thursdays and Saturdays, but by 1934 he was providing daily services over the route and, in April of that year, he began a daily through working from Castlederg to Enniskillen via Omagh. The bus left Castlederg at 1030 hrs and was due in Enniskillen at 1245 hrs and it started on its return journey at 1415 hrs. By that time his buses were providing four double workings between Omagh and Enniskillen, two of which went via Trillick and the others travelled through Irvinestown, the journey time by either route being about 1hr 15mins. The Fleetwing buses had cream bodies with red waist-bands and black roofs and, at the NIRTB take-over, the company owned five buses (1 Bedford; 1 Dennis; 2 Guy; 1 Reo).

118. Simpson's Fleetwing Bus Service at time of takeover by the NIRTB in 1935. William A Simpson is the tall man second from left. He bought a Shell garage in the Ballyholme area of Bangor with his 'bus money'. UFTM L3724/9

During the winter of 1929/30 W F Hill of Omagh, along with Miss Marlowe, also from Omagh, began to run a 20-seater Reo between Omagh, Baronscourt and Strabane, but gave it up about two years later when his bus was sold to Mrs Margaret Charlton of Omagh, who was running the *Heather Queen* buses between Omagh and Cookstown and also between Omagh and Gortin. On the former run she usually provided three double workings and had a near-monopoly on the route which ended when her five small buses (2 Bedford; 3 Reo) were taken over by the NIRTB. However, from time to time, she had to face spasmodic competition on the Cookstown run from George Alexander's *Drumshanbo Queen*. This operator's first bus was a small second-hand Bean which arrived early in 1928, but within a year it had been condemned by the authorities and was replaced by a small Morris. Throughout his time on the road he was usually in trouble with the licencing authorities about the mechanical state of his vehicle and for travelling on routes for which it had not been licenced. Although the *Drumshanbo Queen* was licenced to run on market days between Donaghmore and Cookstown, it seemed to go anywhere its owner pleased. Indeed, a police report of August 1931 states 'he appears at present to have a roving commission over any, and every, road in the area.' Mrs Charlton used to complain about him, but the authorities seem to have been unable to resolve her troubles until Alexander retired in 1932. However, some years later, it was revealed that Alexander was too kind-hearted to be a successful entrepreneur and would always issue tickets to passengers who promised to pay him next day, but seldom did! Furthermore, he never hesitated to take those, without transport of their own, to local fairs or

119. NIRTB buses lined up at Ormeau Park, Belfast for press photo, 30 September 1935. Many vehicles are ex BOC. Photographer A R Hogg. Courtesy B Boyle. UFTM L3779/3

children for a day at the seaside, services for which many of his customers 'forgot' to pay him.

In its early days the principal routes of the NIRTB were worked mainly by 36-seater, petrol-engined buses which were manned by a driver and a conductor. The latter issued pre-printed tickets which had to be punched in the presence of the passenger shortly after he or she had boarded the bus by a door toward the rear of the vehicle. Today, buses on similar routes are normally diesel-engined, can accommodate between 60 and 70 passengers and have a crew of one. Since the entrance is toward the front of the bus, each passenger as he enters has to pay the driver who issues a ticket on which details of the fare and journey have just been printed by a ticket issuing machine. On minor routes the same procedure of ticket issue is followed, but the buses involved are often 25-seaters whereas in 1935 they would have been 14-seaters, the reason being that buses seat-

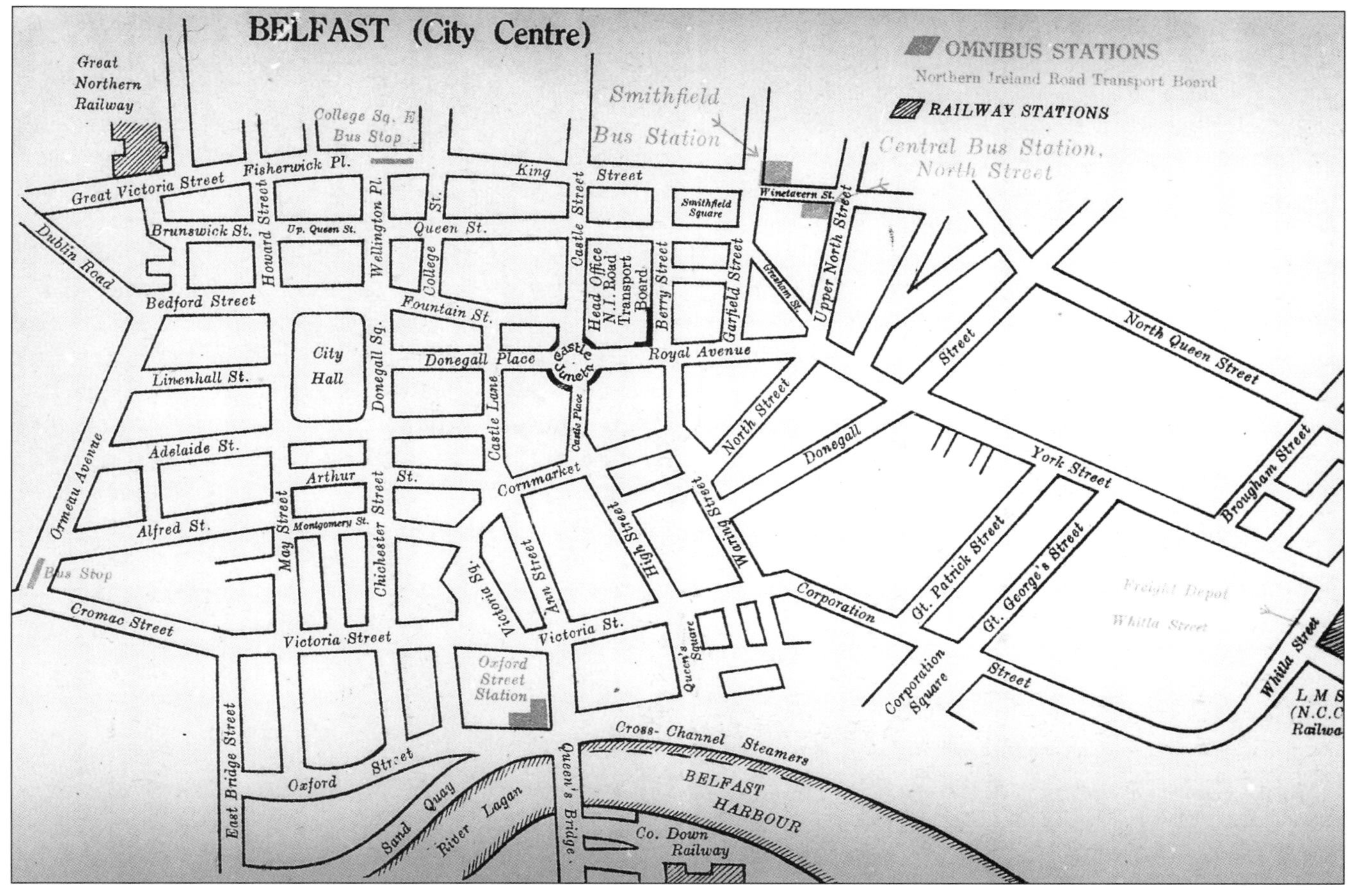

120. NIRTB map of bus and railway stations in Belfast, June 1937. UFTM L3789/1

ing 14, or fewer, passengers were not required to carry a conductor.

REFERENCES

1 *Larne Times,* 3 April 1926
2 Baird's Belfast ABC Railway and Bus Guide 1927
3 *Newtownards Chronicle*, 11 February 1924; PRONI UTA 12/CGA/154
4 *Belfast Topics*, July 1928
5 Communication, Miss M Shilliday
6 *Belfast Telegraph*, 21 January 1927
7 *Mourne Observer*, 19 October 1974
8 Communication, Mr Patrick Downey
9 Communication, Mrs E M Clarke
10 *Belfast Telegraph*, 29 March 1927
11 Sprinks, N W, Sligo, Leitrim & Northern Counties Railway, p 140 (London, 1970)
12 Communication, W Montgomery
13 *Londonderry Sentinel*, 1 June 1912
14 *Londonderry Sentinel*, 28 May 1927
15 *Coleraine Chronicle*, 25 April 1925; 19 September 1927
16 *Belfast Telegraph*, 2 March 1927
17 PRONI UTA/CGA/176
18 Henry File (UFTM E2/12)

8. Private Hire and Touring

The majority of the omnibus proprietors in the province derived a substantial part of their income from touring and private hire work. Some of those engaged in this had long-term contracts for the provision of the transport required by local package tour operators, thus package tour guests staying in Hall's Hotel in Antrim were always taken to Portrush and other places of interest in the buses and charabancs owned by S Girvan of Ballyclare. Indeed, some of these bus owners such as J Gaston of Belfast, S S Henry of Portstewart and the O'Neills of Bangor, who had been engaged in this type of work for several decades, had owned, what were by Irish standards, large bus fleets. This chapter includes the names of the local public service vehicle operators who derived the greater part of their incomes from tour operating as well as descriptions of the businesses of those who owned comparatively large bus fleets during the early 1930s.

R Fallows

R Fallows owned a general merchant business in Dungiven and, between October 1929 and the end of 1934, ran a 14-seater Chevrolet on a thrice-weekly service between Dungiven and Garvagh. He always wanted to run a daily service to Limavady, or some other town not too far away, but was continually refused permission to do so by the Ministry of Home Affairs, no doubt because there were already operators providing satisfactory services on these routes. In the returns published by the government, Fallows was described as a tour operator so it is probable he also ran trips to the seaside during the summer months.

John Gaston

John Gaston of Templemore Avenue, in east Belfast, began to run motor charabancs shortly after the end of the 1914-18 War and, in the summer of 1921, ran a 16-seater pneumatic-tyred, Panhard to Portrush and the Glens of Antrim as well as providing an hourly charabanc service between Belfast and Bangor on Sunday afternoons. He also ran a 12s tour to Copeland Island on which his patrons were given a charabanc ride to Donaghadee, a motor-boat crossing to the island and high tea in Donaghadee on their return.[1] Like many other bus operators he became involved in the Belfast Bus War and got into trouble with the authorities when he continued to run his buses in competition with the trams after the official end of the conflict[2] on 17 December 1928. In May 1929 he acquired the three AECs which T McClements had been running between Belfast and Holywood, but within a few months, he disposed of them to the BCDR, after which he continued in private-hire and touring until 1935 when the NIRTB took over his 20 buses (6 ADC; 4 Dennis; 8 Leyland; 2 Morris), seven of which were less than three years old. The compensation he received, £29,484, was the largest cash payment made by the NIRTB, other operators receiving payments of similar, or larger, amounts usually had to accept part of their compensation in NIRTB stock.

S Girvan

S Girvan of Ballyclare obtained his first charabanc immediately after the end of the 1914-18 War and, in 1923, purchased three Crossley tenders from the police which he rebuilt as 20-seater charabancs. He was interested mainly in private-hire work and for many years held contracts with local hotels, such as Hall's in Antrim, to provide their guests with bus tours to places of interest during their stay in the province.[3] Girvan seems never to have been involved in providing services on recognised bus routes despite the fact that his father had, at one time, run a horse-drawn coach between Ballynure and Belfast. At the NIRTB take-over he owned ten buses (1 Bedford; 3 Crossley; 1 Daimler; 5 Dennis).

D McLarnon

D McLarnon of Belfast, who traded as Hawthorn Tours, provided a useful service for stallholders and other street traders.[4] In 1932 he acquired two Leyland buses which were timed to leave Belfast in the early morning with a complement of small traders and their wares bound for one of the mar-

121. S Girvan's Daimler charabanc. R Ludgate Collection. UFTM L4079/4

kets in the province and, at the end of the day, the same bus brought them back home. His service was a great boon to these people for, in those days, few such people owned motor cars or vans and often experienced considerable difficulty in getting themselves and their goods to market by a reasonable hour. However, by 1935, his business required only one bus for, by then, many of his customers had acquired their own (usually secondhand) motor transport. His service was not continued by the NIRTB after they had acquired his 32-seater Leyland bus.

S Pentland

Samuel Pentland began to run a taxi service from Magdela Street, Belfast, in 1921 and soon afterwards acquired some charabancs which he used mainly for private-hire work.[4] He was a great believer in the efficiency of small operators and the hand-outs advertising his hire facilities usually carried a slogan asking support from all operators against the 'bus monopoly'. In 1935 his six buses (1 AEC; 1 Gilford; 1 Gotfredson; 3 Dennis) were taken over by the NIRTB.

Pioneer, Express and Tonic Buses

These buses were owned by the O'Neill family of Bangor and were engaged mainly in touring and private-hire work.

The Pioneer Motor Tours were the property of Jacob O'Neill who owned a posting and undertaking establishment in Bangor. He acquired his first motor charabanc in 1913 and, for a time, was a partner in The Express Motor Company. By the early 1920s, he had built up a substantial touring business and was also working local bus services to Ballymaconnell, Donaghadee and Groomsport. In 1927/28 he decided to concentrate on touring and sold over half his buses (6 Crossley; 3 Dennis; 2 Renault) to his brother J H

122. Jacob O'Neill's charabanc at the rear of houses in Dufferin Avenue, Bangor. O'Neill stabled his buses in Central Avenue in a building which later became the Little Theatre. UFTM L1459/8

O'Neill for £4000. After this he continued as a tour operator until the NIRTB took over his eight remaining buses (7 Dennis; 1 Gilford). No standard livery seems to have been used for his buses; originally some were red, and later several of them were grey.

123. Pioneer Motor Tours Dennis Lancet bus at Bridge Street, Bangor. Pioneer buses were owned by Jacob O'Neill of Dufferin Avenue, Bangor. UFTM L1931/6

In the same year as the Pioneer buses took to the road, the Express Motor Company began to run short bus trips from Bangor and Belfast. In 1914 it commenced a short lived summer charabanc service between Belfast and Donaghadee[5] via Helen's Bay, Crawfordsburn and the Coast Road between Bangor and Donaghadee, which was advertised as the 'scenic route'. Eleven years later he began another short-lived bus service, which competed with the trains of the BCDR for the Belfast-Comber traffic by charging 'cut-throat' prices, namely 6d by bus compared with 1s by rail for the 8-mile journey. In May 1926 the company, which had been incorporated as a private limited liability company in 1920, went into voluntary liquidation thereby enabling Jacob O'Neill to have more time in which to oversee his Pioneer Tours. However, shortly afterwards he

124. Imperial Bus Service which operated in the North Down and Ards peninsula area. R Ludgate Collection

transferred the non-touring interest of his business to his brother J H O'Neill who used it as the nucleus of his own company which traded as the Tonic Buses.

It was not long before the Tonic Buses became the fifth largest bus operator in Ulster and in 1935 the NIRTB acquired his 25 buses (1 Albion; 2 Commer; 6 Dennis; 3 Laffley; 2 Renault; 10 Reo; 1 Thornycroft), which varied in age from a 14-seater Reo Sprinter of 1923 to a 32-seater Commer of 1932. Originally the Tonic Buses were painted dark blue but this was eventually changed to purple during the early 1930s. J H O'Neill, himself, entered the road transport business in the early 1920s by starting a taxi service in Bangor and, shortly afterwards began to run local bus services between Bangor, Groomsport and Donaghadee as well as operating his half-day tours from Bangor. In 1928 he began to compete with the BOC for the Bangor-Newtownards traffic, his buses travelling via the Six Road Ends whereas his rival went by the direct route through Conlig. Within the next three years he had strengthened his position on the Donaghadee and Groomsport roads by purchasing the three small Chevrolets which the Imperial BS had been running between Bangor and Donaghadee. In addition, he acquired the three 16-seater Overland buses with which the well-established Groomsport grocer, J Heyburn Smyth, had been operating the Coaster Bus Service between Bangor and Groomsport since 1921.[6] The Tonic Bus Service continued to expand and in 1934 it was then working a quarter-hour service between Bangor and Groomsport as well as a half-hour service between Bangor and Ballymaconnell. Although the name Tonic went into disuse at the NIRTB take-over, it was revived soon afterwards, for some of the money received by the O'Neill's for their transport undertakings was invested in the building of a cinema in Hamilton Road, Bangor, which they named the Tonic. Later the name was changed to the Odeon. However, dwindling numbers led to the closure of the cinema and the building was finally demolished during the mid-1990s.

R Owens, M Sawey, W Sloan

At the time of the NIRTB take-over these operators were providing day tours and private-hire facilities. Owens and Sloan worked from Belfast and Sawey from Newcastle. Sloan was the owner of five buses (2 Gilford; 3 Leyland) whilst Owens and Sawey had three, the former possessing a Halley Conqueror and two Daimler and the latter two Lancia and one Guy.

White Star Line Tours

In the mid-1920s, W Stewart of Belfast formed the White Star Line Tours which, in 1928, usually ran day and afternoon excursions from Oxford Street in Belfast. Oxford Street was also the terminal of many of the bus services from Bangor, Donaghadee and Portaferry and Stewart was often in trouble with the police for his crews would frequently try to entice travellers intending to use these buses to go by Stewart's touring coaches instead. In 1935 he owned eight buses (1 ADC; 1 Dennis; 6 Leyland), six of which were over five years old.

Other Tour Operators

Many of the smaller operators derived most of their livelihoods from day trips and charter work. During the early 1930s six of these were one-bus owners, viz Dickson & Ireland, Belfast; F Johnston, Larne; H & K Mallagh, Belfast; A W Pithers, Newcastle; W Ramsey, Lisburn; J Shank, Belfast. Only two – P Murphy, Ballymena and C Robinson, Larne possessed two buses. In addition the Fawcetts, who operated package tours from their hotels in Antrim and Portrush, chartered buses from the railways. Buses so employed carried the name Fawcett prominently displayed on a facia on their roofs immediately above their windscreen.

REFERENCES

1 *Belfast Telegraph*, 17 June 1921
2 *Belfast Newsletter*, 19 December 1928
3 Communication, Dr S Girvan
4 Communication, D McLarnon and S Pentland
5 *Newtownards Chronicle*, 7 July 1914
6 *Bangor Spectator*, 14 June 1921

Pentland's Coaches

Sun Saloon & All-Weather Coaches

32, 34, 36 SEATERS.

5/6 Seater Saloon Cars for Private Hire.

12 MAGDALA STREET and SUNWICH ST., RAVENHILL AVENUE, BELFAST.

Phones 5614 & 5204.

9. Other Bus Services

The road transport services owned by Belfast Corporation, and those in Counties Donegal, Cavan and Monaghan were exempt from the provisions of the 1935 Road and Railways (Northern Ireland) Act, and therefore remained outside the NIRTB. Nevertheless, the development of road passenger services followed similar lines on both sides of the border. In the beginning a few operators would put one or two small buses on the road. As time went on, the more prosperous either absorbed or, by providing more reliable services, drove their competitors off the road. Ultimately, all the remaining local operators became part of the large public utilities which today dominate passenger services throughout the whole of Ireland. Thus, in Cavan, Monaghan and South Donegal, Bus Éireann has now a monopoly of the passenger traffic but, in the north and north-west of Donegal, all passenger road services are worked by the Lough Swilly Bus Service.

Counties Antrim, Armagh and Down

Belfast City

Belfast Corporation began to run motor buses in 1926 when two town services were introduced and, from this small beginning, its bus services have grown until, today, all public transport in the city is provided by buses. On 4 October 1926 it began a service between the Cavehill Road and the city centre and, a month later, commenced operating a cross-town route between the Gas Works (Ormeau Road) and Agnes Street (Crumlin Road) via Donegall Pass and Albert Street. Both routes were worked by 30-seater AEC buses which had been obtained by the corporation a few weeks previously. Two more buses (32-seater ADC) were purchased in 1928 and, in December of that year, the corporation became the reluctant owners of over 50 buses, which private operators had been running during the 1928

125. BCT AEC bus Fleet No. 1 Reg XI 7331 with body by Short Bros of Rochester. The photograph was probably taken on the first day of operation – 4 October 1926. UFTM L477/1

126. The first BCT motor bus at Henderson Avenue Terminus, Cavehill, Belfast. The City Hall – Cavehill Road route carried Route No. 1, and this AEC bus was given the Fleet No. 1. Date, October 1926. UFTM L1529/9

Bus War; some of these were truly ancient such as a 14-seater Renault of 1914 vintage.

The Bus War had been brought about by the passing of the 1926 Motor Vehicles (Traffic and Regulation) NI Act. In this the authority to licence public service vehicles was transferred from local authorities to the Northern Ireland Ministry of Home Affairs. This meant that local government bodies, such as Belfast Corporation, no longer had the powers to protect their transport systems by refusing to grant licences for services within their boundaries, an anomaly which had apparently escaped the notice of private bus owners throughout the province until the late spring of 1928.[1] After this discovery they acted quickly, so that in the first week in June the BOC and HMS Catherwood began to run buses in competition with the trams within the city boundary. Their lead was immediately followed by other bus operators so that, by August, there were at least 20 private omnibus proprietors running well over a 100 buses in the city. The corporation responded by cutting fares, and even contemplated getting a large bus fleet of its own so that every privately owned bus would be shadowed by a corporation one, thus repeating the tactic whereby every tram had been accompanied by a private bus, which tried to get to each stopping place just ahead of the tram. However, throughout the summer, discussions were taking place between the corporation, the government and the bus operators. In November they came to an agreement whereby the bus operators renounced their claims to traffic solely within the City of Belfast and conceded the principle that the corporation had the exclusive right to traffic within an area extending to a quarter of a mile beyond the city boundary. Furthermore, the interests of

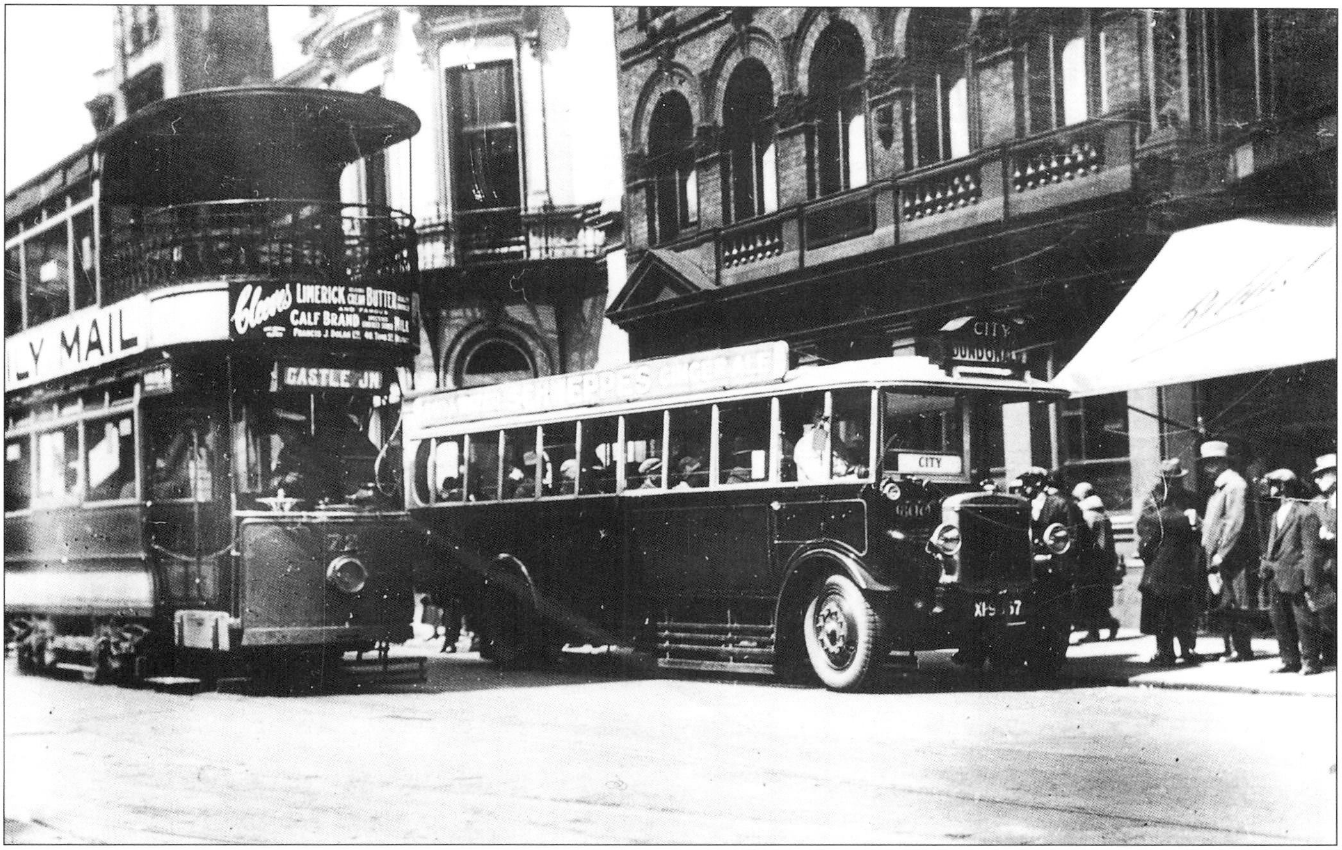

127. BOC Associated Daimler Co bus and BCT tram No. 72 at Castle Place, Belfast during the 1928 Bus War. UFTM L1529/8

operators elsewhere in Northern Ireland would be protected in that there would be a limit to the number of licences issued by the government, who undertook to issue no new licences in respect of any route so long as it was satisfied that an adequate service was being maintained by the people authorised to operate it. Agreement was also reached that the regulations should come into force within the city on 17 December 1928 and that a datum line for routes elsewhere in Northern Ireland should be fixed, retrospectively, as 27 August of that year. This last clause meant that all operators running buses outside Belfast on 27 August 1928 had to register their buses, routes, timetables and fares with the Ministry of Home Affairs, a registration which has provided transport historians with a wealth of information which used to be available in the relevant files held in the Public Record Office of Northern Ireland.

128. BCT Falls Road depot. The bus in the background is probably Leyland PLSC 1 Reg XI 8007, an ex HMS Catherwood vehicle which was new in 1927. It was later converted into a tower wagon. Date, early 1930s. UFTM L1615/9

129. Bus competing with trams at Royal Avenue, Belfast, 10 September 1928. Belfast Telegraph *Collection. UFTM L3531/8*

The corporation also agreed to compensate those operators who had ordered buses to work the renumerative routes they had hoped to operate in the city. This was carried out by purchasing 51 of the buses from 16 of the many operators who had been involved in the Bus War. Thus 18 buses were purchased from Catherwood, 10 from the Imperial BS, 5 from F H Nelson and, at the other end of the scale, 10 proprietors had to be content with selling only one bus each.

Despite the agreement for the withdrawal of private bus operators from tramway routes on Monday 17 December, a few private buses attempted to continue working in the city,[2] but the traffic department of the Royal Ulster Constabulary was particularly vigilant so that all but one of the operators had come off the streets by the end of the week. The exception was W J Clements who had come to an arrangement with the Corporation that he would continue to run 'The Major' bus service between the city centre and Gilnahirk via the Upper Newtownards Road, Sandown Road and Cherryvalley. As Gilnahirk was about half a mile beyond the city boundary, it was argued that the buses concerned should have been classified as running to a destination outside the city and should, therefore, be permitted to continue operating normally, provided they did not compete with municipally owned transport within the city boundary. However, because a considerable part of the route followed by the Major Buses within the city was over roads on which there were no trams, they were permitted to take up, or set down, fare paying passengers at any recognised stopping place en route. Similar exemptions were also given, at a later date, to William Scott and to McCreight and Ross, who ran buses to the Drumbo district which were also permitted to take up and set down passengers on the Malone and Ormeau Roads in Belfast, subject in their cases, to the restriction that the passengers concerned should be charged a minimum fare of 4d. In addition to working the Gilnahirk service, Clements was much involved in private-hire work and his buses, no matter how employed, had the reputation of being the best maintained public service vehicles in the province, indeed, there was always a waiting list to buy his discarded buses, some of which were purchased by the Londonderry & Lough Swilly Railway. The arrangement between Clements and the corporation stipulated that he would provide the buses and crews, for which he would be paid on a mileage basis, and the corporation would keep the fares. This seems to have been particularly satisfactory, for not only did Clements pay his men higher wages than they would have got if they had been corporation employees, but his service cost the corporation a few coppers per mile less than if it had to run its own buses.[3] The Gilnahirk service continued to be worked by Clements until ill health made it necessary to transfer his blue buses to the corporation in 1947. A year later he died having never run a bus on a Sunday; a day on which Gilnahirk was served by Belfast Corporation buses.

The corporation acquired no new buses in 1929 but, toward the end of 1930, it purchased six 52-seater Leyland TD1 double-deckers which went into service in December of that year. More buses were acquired in 1932, 1934 and 1935 so that, by 1 January 1936, it owned about 70 buses, 60 having been acquired since 1930. About half of the new buses were double-deckers (15 Leyland; 10 AEC; 5 Daimler) with accommodation for 52 passengers, and the remainder were 32-seater single-deckers, mainly Dennis.[4]

130. Belfast Corporation Shelvoke and Drewry passenger vehicle Reg AZ 5450 at Bellevue Zoo and Pleasure Gardens. The transverse engine was housed to the right of the driver who sat above the gearbox. Its makers claimed the vehicle was 'so simple it can be driven by a labourer'. R Ludgate Collection

During the 1929 Christmas holidays the corporation began to run buses to supplement the trams on some of the longer routes. The buses generally ran at 20-minute intervals whereas the trams provided a five-minute service. The buses were considerably faster and were favoured by those travelling to the outer suburbs who preferred to pay the slightly higher fares and shorten the journey time. Thus passengers going to Dundonald paid 3d if travelling by bus compared with 2d on the trams, but their journey from the city centre to the terminus took about 25 minutes which was some 10 minutes less than by tram.

In general, the buses were well patronised except on the road to Cregagh on which the bus service was withdrawn on 3 October 1932. This was balanced by the opening of new routes from the city centre to Oldpark and the Crumlin Road later in the same year.

In the 1930s the buses owned by the corporation used the same livery as the trams, blue and cream; this colour scheme had been adopted in 1929, previous to which all the trams had been painted in the same style as had been used by the city's trams in Victorian times, red and cream.

Coastal Bus Service: Sureline Coaches

In the years following the setting up of the NIRTB the government was most sparing in its issue of new operating licences to bus operators. However, in the mid-1960s the system was relaxed and tenders were invited from private individuals who wished to take over the operations of several of the less renumerative routes. After some delay the Coastal Bus Service and Sureline Coaches were licenced to operate buses in the Ballycastle, Portrush, Coleraine Triangle and in the vicinity of Lurgan. The Coastal BS took over the working of UTA Services 136 and 141 on 25 April 1966 and on 6 May of the same year Sureline Coaches began to operate six bus routes in the Lurgan area, several of which served the new town of Craigavon. Unfortunately, the population of the area failed to expand as expected, and this, and the general uncertainty due to the political unrest, led to the company handing back its services to Ulsterbus in the late 1980s. Early in its career the company had abandoned the issue of weekly and monthly return tickets in favour of multiple-journey ones, one of the first bus companies in the British Isles to adopt this idea. The Coastal BS was also seriously affected by the falling away of the tourist traffic due to the Troubles and on 10 May 1974 Ulsterbus took over the working of the former UTA Services Nos 136 and 141. At one time each of these proprietors had been heavily involved in touring and private-hire when the Coastal BS owned 16 buses and Sureline Coaches owned 26.

Counties Cavan and Monaghan

During the 1930s the total population of Counties Cavan and Monaghan was about 140,000, about the same as that of County Londonderry. The largest urban centre was Monaghan town, with a population of about 5000. Since there was little industry in the area, the outlook for the development of financially viable transport businesses was not promising. Nevertheless, bus services on a modest scale were developed in both counties.

In Monaghan there was a growth of private bus companies in the autumn of 1927. In November of that year the editorial in the *Northern Standard* commented: 'within the last few months, nearly every road in County Monaghan has been linked up with principal towns by a bus service!' The first service was owned by F H Nelson and linked Ballybay, Monaghan, Middletown and Armagh. There were three double-workings each day. Nelson later extended his service to Castleblayney. In December, Fairways Limited introduced a service from Monaghan to Dublin. The Nugent Bus Service competed with Nelson serving many of the same towns and also running to Carrickmacross, Shercock, Bailieboro' and Cavan. Boyds ran a service from Clones to Monaghan. Jimmy Parkes of Castleblayney operated the Classic Bus Service between Monaghan, Castleblayney, Carrickmacross and Dundalk. In 1929 Maurice Cassidy's Erne Bus Service began to operate from Enniskillen to Clones, Newbliss and Cootehill. He extended his service to Cavan in 1930. In 1929 the GNR began to operate buses in Monaghan, this immediately drew a protest from the private operators. Parkes and Nugent tried to get Monaghan County Council to protest at the GNR's action but by the outbreak of the Second World War in 1939 all but one of the private operators had either been absorbed into the GNR or gone out of business (see chapter 5). The operator who retained his independence was Henry Cassidy of Scotstown whose cream and green buses provided a service between Monaghan town and Scotstown for many years.[5]

County Donegal

With the exception of that part of the county to the east of Letterkenny and Stranorlar, Donegal is one of the most sparsely-populated parts of Ireland. During the railway era the main purveyors of public transport were the County Donegal and the Londonderry and Lough Swilly Railways. Both of these were narrow gauge (3ft) lines and each worked about 100 miles of track. On the CDR the stations were situated in, or near, the places they served, whereas on the LLSR it would seem that stations had been placed as far as possible from the villages whose names they bore. Consequently, the two companies met the challenge from the road in different ways. The CDR by concentrating on improving its economic efficiency with initiatives such as the introduction of railcars which stopped at level crossings on request; the LLSR decided that its passenger traffic could be more expeditiously handled by running its own buses.

The CDR, like its neighbour the LLSR, at one time ran a bus service as part of its effort to increase passenger traffic. In 1929 it approached the Ministry of Commerce in Dublin for approval to open three short bus routes which could act as feeders for its system.[6] Approval was granted, but the railway had not the funds available either to buy, or hire, the necessary buses. However, in 1930 it managed to purchase three somewhat run-down buses which had at one time been owned by James Bleakney of Portadown. For the next three years the buses ran between Killybegs and Glenties via Ardara, but the roads were so atrocious, that by then the buses were completely worn out. The GNR came to the rescue and worked the service on behalf of the CDR and, for the next 40 years, continued to provide replacement bus services on those sections of the CDR railway network from which passenger services have been withdrawn. However, this passed to CIE in 1971 and today is provided by its direct successor, Bus Éireann.

The Londonderry & Lough Swilly Railway served north-west Donegal. The first section of the railway, that between Derry and Farland Point, was opened on 31 December 1863 and, 40 years later, its trains were running between Derry, Carndonagh and Burtonport and its steamships were plying between Fahan and the small harbour on Lough Swilly.[7] In 1929 the company decided that the future of its passenger traffic was on the road rather than on rail and, over the next three years, it built up a fleet of over 30 buses by buying out nine operators and by purchasing five new vehicles from Leyland Motors.

Despite the bad roads in the north-west, the LLSR buses provided a faster and more frequent service than that given by its trains. Thus, in 1930, Gweedore was served by three buses each day from Derry, which took an average time of just over three hours, whereas the company's two mixed trains required at least four hours for the same journey.

On 26 September 1929, the LLSR made its initial move into road passenger transport by purchasing four buses (3 Graham-Dodge; 1 Leyland) from Edward Barr of Buncrana. The railway paid £1700 in cash and, in return, it received the buses and assumed the responsibility for paying off any instalments still outstanding on the vehicles. During the next twelve months the LLSR purchased ten buses from four operators, as well as obtaining five new Leyland 32-seater buses. Five of the second-hand buses (2 Gilford; 3 Reo) had belonged to John Doherty of Buncrana, three buses (1 Graham-Dodge; 2 Guy) came from Samuel Burns of Kilmacrennan, the remaining two belonged to J Kane of Culdaff (14-seater Morris) and Daniel McLaughlin of Carndonagh (26-seater Albion).

The railway's largest acquisition was made toward the end of 1931 when it bought, at a cost of £19,200, the 17 buses which James Winter had got together to form the County Donegal Motor Service in May of that year. Despite each bus having been individually licenced by the Northern Ireland Government to work between the Donegal Border and Derry City, there was a long delay before the CDMS as a corporate body received its operating licence. Indeed, the delay was so long that, by the end of the year, Winter had sold his company to the LLSR, given up all his bus interests and soon became a successful property developer in Belfast. His CDMS venture had involved four operators, Joseph Doherty of Moville (1 Chevrolet; 3 Reo), Daniel Kearney of Malin (2 Reo), Ward Bros of Kerrykeel (1 Leyland; 5 Reo; 1 Thornycroft) and Roberts Bros of Foyle Road, Derry (3 Chevrolet; 1 Reo).

131. Joseph Doherty's Reo FBX bus Reg IH 2753. This bus was new in 1929 and was acquired by J Winter of the CDMS in May 1931. It then went to the LLSR at the end of 1931. UFTM L1528/1.

In 1932, seven, almost new, 32-seater Vulcan buses were purchased from Steele and Ferguson of Glasgow, two of which had bodies built by HMS Catherwood. Thus in about four years the LLSR had acquired over 35 serviceable buses which enabled it to operate a larger mileage of bus routes than that of its rail track. However, the change did not always proceed smoothly, for in the spring of 1931, the buses running to Dungloe had to be terminated at Gortahork, about 20 miles short of their destination because of the deplorable state of the road and a threat from Donegal County Council that legal proceedings would be taken to recover the cost of the damage done to its roads by the LLSR buses. By its acquisition of the CDMS, the LLSR became the owner of the oldest regularly operated bus route in the north-west. This connected Derry with Moville and had been worked by Roberts Bros of Derry since its opening on 1 June 1912. (See page 96). Until about 1928 the Roberts' only competitors on this route had been the paddle steamers *Lady Clare*, *Cynthia* and *Cragbue* which had plied,

132. Lough Swilly Railway Vulcan Prince bus Reg GE 5529. It was originally owned by Steel & Ferguson of Glasgow. Date of photograph, 1933. Charles Friel Collection. Courtesy Real Photographs x 4949. UFTM L3800/1

133. Hugh, Reginald and Charles Roberts with their Lacre buses at the Guildhall, Derry in 1913. During the First World War they operated a bus to Limavady which was powered by town gas. UFTM L3722/13

somewhat intermittently, between Derry and Moville during this period. However, in the summer of 1928, Joseph Doherty, who owned a

134. Lacre bus Reg. UI 92 belonging to Roberts Bros of Derry. This photograph first appeared in Irish Life *magazine captioned 'Signs of the Times – a new motor mail omnibus in Londonderry'. Date, 1912. Courtesy C Flewitt. UFTM L3722/13*

garage in Moville, began running rival buses over the 19-mile route between Derry and Moville which provided several round trips with an average journey time of 1hr 10min and a single fare costing 1s 9d. Unfortunately, his buses seem to have been kept in poor mechanical condition and his service had not the reliability of the Roberts' service.

The busiest bus route out of Derry was, and still is, that to the seaside resort of Buncrana. On 21 June 1926 Edward Barr began to run a bus over the route and, shortly afterwards, John Doherty of Buncrana started a rival service with his Swilly Queen Buses, the advertisements for which were headed 'Travel by the Swilly Queen, bus every hour.' By 1928 both operators were providing an hourly service with their buses scheduled to cover the 14 miles in 45 minutes, a time which took into account the average delays occasioned by stops for customs examination at the

135. McMonagle's horse-drawn long car (Bian). This vehicle ran between Strand Road (opposite the Londonderry and Lough Swilly Railway terminus) and Waterloo Place (opposite the Northern Counties Hotel). It served Derry city for 50 years ceasing in April 1931. Mr McMonagle is holding the reins. Date, c.1920. Photographer W A Green. UFTM WAG 3343

border. In July 1929 both operators agreed to operate a fixed interval service in which Doherty's buses left each terminal on the hour and Barr's at the half hour. This arrangement ended in November 1929 when Barr was taken over by the LLSR, a fate which overtook Doherty in July 1930. Just as in their day, holiday traffic over this route can often be very heavy and, on summer Sundays, buses still leave either terminal just as soon as they are full. The only bus which operated in the Buncrana area which was never taken over by the LLSR was a Vulcan 14-seater owned by James Galbraith of Buncrana.

During the late 1920s, some of the Derry-Buncrana buses began to continue their journeys to Carndonagh and Malin Head. These places were also served by LLSR buses which travelled over the same road between Derry and Quigley's Point as the Derry-Moville buses, after which they branched northward to Carndonagh. In 1927 Daniel Kearney of Malin began operating over this route and was joined by Daniel McLaughlin's *Blue Bird* bus a few years later. The third private operator on this route was J Kane of Culdaff whose bus also served his home town. The businesses of these three operators were ultimately acquired by the LLSR.

The service ultimately operated by the LLSR in north-west Donegal began with a twice-daily service between Kerrykeel and Derry which was started by Ward Bros of Kerrykeel[8] in June 1927. One of their buses left Kerrykeel at 0815 hrs and, after passing through Letterkenny and Manorcunningham, was due at the Guildhall in Derry at 1045 hrs; the return workings left the city at 1630 hrs. The afternoon bus ran from

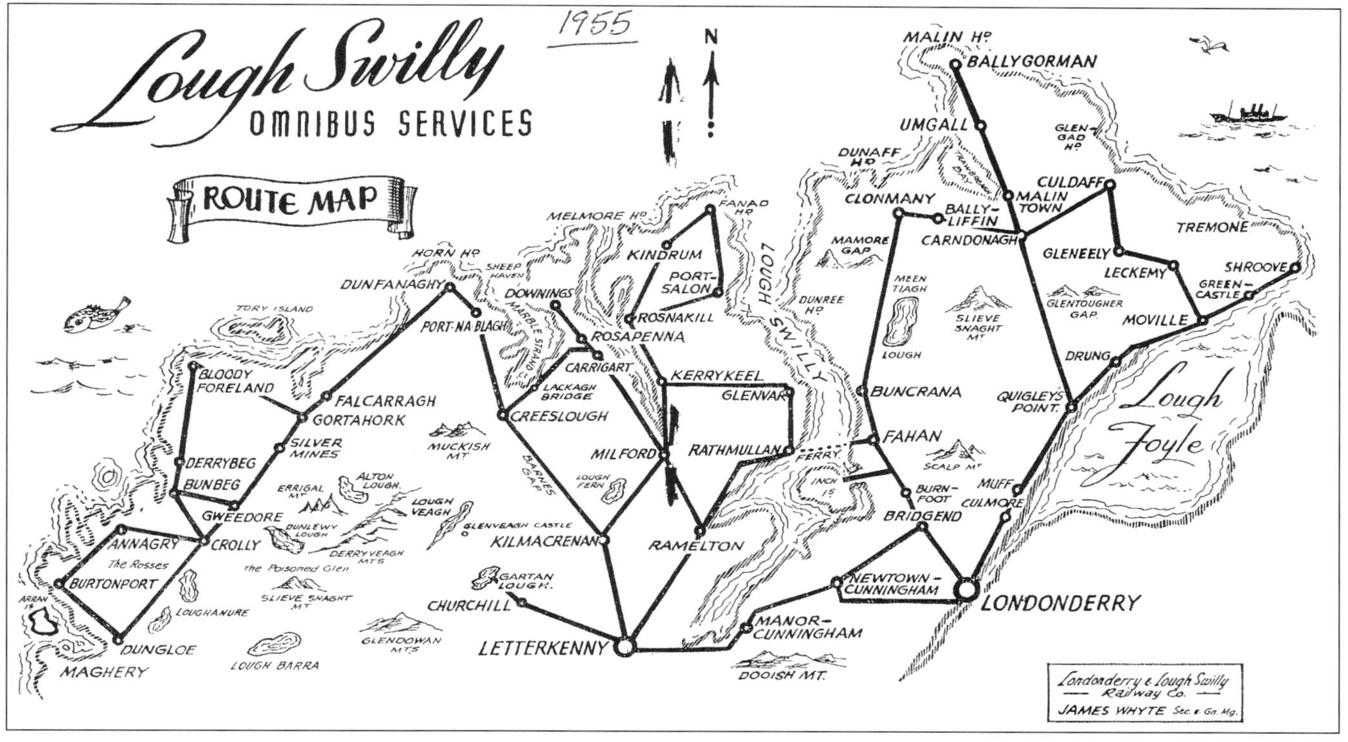

136. Map of Lough Swilly bus services, 1955. UFTM.

Downings and, after spending the night in Derry, departed on its return journey at 0900 hrs. In July 1929 the Wards acquired the 20-seater Reo which Patrick Coyle, also from Kerrykeel, had used on occasions to help them out. Later in the same month they purchased the goodwill of Patrick Kelly's bus service based in Kilmacrennan. By the late 1920s, the Ward buses were also running twice daily between Derry and Dungloe near Burtonport, which connect at Letterkenny with buses for Downings and Port Salon. The other major operator in the north-west was Samuel Burns of Kilmacrennan who went into business in July 1928 by running buses, in conjunction with the Wards, to Dungloe as well as competing with the trains of the CDR for the Strabane-Letterkenny traffic.

By mid-1932 the LLSR had attained a monopoly of the road passenger services in Inishowen and north-west Donegal and were continuing to provide the same type of service as that which had been run by the operators whom they had taken over. The complete closure of its railway on 10 August 1953 did not affect its passenger road services for, by that time, very few passengers travelled by train. However, it now meant that the LLSR was still a railway company, much involved in the transport business, but possessing neither track nor trains. This anomaly ended on 1 April 1981 when it was purchased by Patrick Doherty, a London property developer who originally came from Buncrana. However, for several decades before this, the LLSR had been trading as the Lough Swilly Omnibus Service.

The LLSR had its headquarters and passenger station at Pennyburn on the outskirts of Derry, but its buses usually worked from Great James Street where the company provided a waiting room. In 1934 it possessed 34 single decker buses of nine different makes, but steps were already being taken to standardise its fleet by restricting the purchase of new vehicles to Leylands. During the seven years covered in this account the LLSR never owned a double-decker and all its buses were painted in a sombre livery of dark brown with black panels, a colour scheme which was

137. NCC Albion PX 65 bus Reg AZ 7756 with body by Alexander. New in 1931. UFTM L3236/11

brightened some years later by the substitution of ivory for black in the company's colour scheme.

REFERENCES

1 Greer, P E, *Road Versus Rail*, c3 (Belfast 1983)
2 *Belfast News Letter*, 19 December 1928
3 Communication, H Clements
4 Belfast Corporation Transport, PSV Circle (London 1962)
5 Livingstone, P, *The Monaghan Story*, Clogher Historical Society (Enniskillen 1980).
6 Dougherty, H, *The Bus Services of the County Donegal Railways* (Dublin, 1973)
7 Patterson, E M, *The Lough Swilly Railway* (Newton Abbot, 1960); Thompson, K M, *Lough Swilly's 50 Years* (Derry 1981)
8 *Londonderry Sentinel*, 9 June 1927

Acknowledgements

A work such as this cannot be compiled without the assistance of others, and the authors wish to thank all who have helped them in the collection of material, especially the staff at the Public Record Office of Northern Ireland, at the Central, Linenhall and Queen's University Libraries in Belfast, and at the headquarters and branch libraries of the North Eastern and South Eastern Education and Library Boards. They also acknowledge with gratitude, the help that has been received from the Ulster Museum, Ulster Folk and Transport Museum, the Federation of Ulster Local Studies, Institute of Irish Studies, Ulsterbus, Northern Ireland Transport Holding Company, Lisburn Museum, Enniskillen Museum, Bangor Heritage Centre, National Library of Ireland, Her Majesty's Stationery Office, Valentine Postcards, Real Photographs, Leyland Motors and Larne Folklore Society.

They would also like to place on record their thanks to B C Boyle, the late R C Ludgate and W H Montgomery for their readiness to share with them their wide knowledge of omnibus services in Ulster. Many others have given generously of their time and knowledge, and the authors would like to express their appreciation of the assistance given by the following: Andrew Anderson, David Blair, Arthur Campbell, H C Casserley, H M S Catherwood, Thomas Charters, H Clements, Michael Collins, A F Cook, Dr W H Crawford, A W Croughton, C D Deane, John Eadie, R Ennis, Tom Ferris, J D Fitzgerald, Clifton Flewitt, Charles Friel, J Gray, P E Greer, Gertrude Hamilton, M Henry, J H Houston, D Lawther, Dr E K Lloyd, H McClatchey, W F McCleery, Aiken McClelland, Mr McClements, Dr W A McCutcheon, B McDonald, R MacDonald, J H McGuigan, Cyril McIntyre, Mrs M McKinney, J McKnight, Very Rev Alfred Martin, W Middleton, W H Milligan, S Miskimmon, S R Moffett, Alfred Montgomery, R L Morrison, D Morrow, Noel Nesbitt, T B O'Loughlin, Mr Osborne, W K Parke, W J Patterson, Paul Rafferty, H W R Robinson, Miss M Shilliday, K M Thompson, R J Troy, C Wallace, A Walsh, D R M Weatherup, Debra Wenlock, Richard Whitford and Ian Wilson.

Finally, they wish to thank Lauraine Lindsay, Maureen Paige and Margaret Pritchard for typing the various manuscripts and inputting the text and tables onto computer, and also the photography department of the Ulster Folk and Transport Museum for producing the prints required.

INDIA.

Travel via a Catherwood Bus and reach your destination in safety—only the best is good enough for H. M. S. Catherwood, Ltd., and all their machines are equipped with the World's Best Tyre—INDIA

INDIA SUPER TYRES (ULSTER) LTD.

34 GLOUCESTER STREET, BELFAST

'PHONE 310

Bibliography

Books

Cummings, J — Railway Motor Buses and Motor Services in the British Isles: Vol 1 (Oxford: 1978)

Currie, J R L — The Northern Counties Railway: Vol 2: (Newton Abbot: 1974)

Dougherty, H — The Bus Services of the County Donegal Railways: (Dublin: 1973)

Greer, P E — Road versus Rail: (Belfast: 1973)

Hibbs, J — The History of British Bus Services: (Newton Abbot: 1969)

Jack, D — The Leyland Bus: (Glossop: 1977)

Livingstone, P — Fermanagh: (Enniskillen: 1969): Monaghan: (Enniskillen: 1980)

Norton and Shaw — Carlingford Lough and County Down: (London: 1878)

McClintock, W — Public Transport in Northern Ireland: (HMSO: 1938)

Millar, G I — Fifty Years of Public Service: (Belfast: 1986)

Patterson, E M — The County Donegal Railways: (Newton Abbot: 1962)

The Lough Swilly Railways: (Newton Abbot: 1964)

Pole, Felix J C — Transport Conditions in Northern Ireland: (HMSO, Belfast: 1934)

Smyth, T S — The Civic History of the Town of Cavan: (Cavan: 1938)

Thomson, K M — Lough Swilly's 50 Years: (Derry: 1979)

Annual Report and Accounts of the Northern Ireland Road Transport Board: 1936–1941 (Belfast)

Publications of the PSV Circle (59 Palmer Road, Cheam, Surrey, SM3 8EF) and the Omnibus Society (The Spinney, Meadow Road, Ashstead, Surrey KT21 1QR)

PI 1 Small Bus and Coach Operators in Ireland: (1964)
PI 2 Córas Iompair Éireann: (1965)
PI 3 Londonderry and Lough Swilly Railway: (1966)
PI 4 Belfast Corporation Transport: (1968)
PI 5 Northern Ireland Road Transport Board: (1972)

Periodicals
Baird's ABC, Belfast
Belfast and Northern Ireland Directory
Interchange (Irish Transport Trust: Belfast)
Modern Transport
Omnibus Magazine

Appendix A

Abbreviations

BCT	Belfast Corporation Transport
BCDR	Belfast & County Down Railway
BNCR	Belfast & Northern Counties Railway
BOC	Belfast Omnibus Company
CDR	County Donegal Railways
CDMS	County Donegal Motor Service
CIE	Córas Iompair Éireann
GNR	Great Northern Railway
GSR	Great Southern Railways
HMSC	HMS Catherwood
IOC	Irish Omnibus Company
LLSR	Londonderry & Lough Swilly Railway
LMS	London Midland and Scottish Railway
MR	Midland Railway
NCC	Northern Counties Committee
NIOC	Northern Ireland Omnibus Company
NIRTB	Northern Ireland Road Transport Board
SLNCR	Sligo Leitrim and Northern Counties Railway
UTA	Ulster Transport Authority

Appendix B

At the formation of the NIRTB in 1935, the omnibus proprietors involved were compensated for their businesses either in cash or in NIRTB Stock. There were three classes of the latter, Northern Ireland Transport 4% A (1970-1995) Stock and Northern Ireland Transport B Stock. At first the A Stock had been divided into two classes known as A1 and A2, but these were merged into a single A Stock in July 1938. The B Stock ranked as ordinary shares, the interest of which could vary from year to year. Shortly after the unification of the A Stock the Board became unable to pay any interest on its capital, and within a few months the Northern Ireland Ministry of Finance decided to purchase all the issued A and B Stock from their holders. The following table has been compiled from information obtained from Ulsterbus, PSV Circle, Omnibus Society and the published accounts of the NIRTB. The former publication also contains fleet lists of the NIRTB, the UTA and Ulsterbus up to the year 1971.

APPENDIX B TABLE: OMNIBUS COMPANIES TAKEN OVER BY THE NIRTB

Number of buses owned and remuneration received by their owners at the NIRTB take-over in 1935.

Company	Vehicles	Consideration Cash (£Sterling)	Stock (Units of £1.00)	
1 October 1935				
Belfast Omnibus Company	169	–	100000	A1
			19041	A2
			271250	B
Belfast & County Down Railway	14	–	8792	A1
			10000	B
Great Northern Railway	50	–	39763	A2
HMS Catherwood	70	–	59395	A1
			41000	B
Northern Counties Committee	131	–	165381	A2
			5000	B
1 November 1935				
W E Hobson, Dungannon	15	5074	8507	A1
			22437	B
Imperial BS, Donaghadee	11	15000	6146	A1
			18854	B
Independent BS, Belfast	8	8387	–	
Wm Irvine & Son, Larne	2	5000	16000	B
Kane Bros, Donaghadee	4	3250	–	
J McCabe, Waringstown	5	5000	–	
J McCartney, Newtownards	9	5000	18464	B
19 November 1935				
W A Agnew, Belfast	2	816	–	
R Barkley, Larne	1	1300	–	
M Clarke & Son, Banbridge (formerly Leitrim)	1	1462	–	
B Cregan, Newry	1	1737	–	
C Downey, Rathfriland	5	4771	–	
D Lawther, Dunmurry	8	2000	2592	A1
			2648	B
J Lawther, Ballywalter	1	3030	352	A1
R Lawther, Ballywalter	2	3756	–	
H McAnulty, Warrenpoint	5	4100	–	
R McGivern, Carrowdore	1	1400	–	
M McNally, Newry	3	1750	–	
J McNeilly, Belfast	4	5000	7535	B
W E Martin, Rathfriland	1	1303	–	
W Nevin, Belfast	3	5159	–	
R Patterson, Belfast	5	12300	–	
J & R Steen, Newtownhamilton	4	4715	–	
R Stevenson & Sons, Rathfriland	6	6760	–	
T V Weir, Newtownards	2	1100	–	
D Wilson, Crumlin	3	3000	–	
J Wilson, Belfast	1	3628	–	

Company	**Vehicles**	**Consideration** **Cash (£Sterling)**	**Stock (Units of £1.00)**	
3 December 1935				
Mrs M Charleton, Omagh	5	11082	–	
W Dow, Belfast	1	2685	–	
W Finlay & Son, Castlewellan	1	2400	–	
S S Henry, Portstewart	9	23000	–	
F Howe, Ballymena	3	1500	–	
J Jamieson, Broughshane	2	2700	–	
W Kerr, Toomebridge	5	5000	9230	B
J McLearnon, Lurgan	2	1300	–	
T Montgomery, Broughshane	2	2800	–	
J H O'Neill, Bangor	25	21400	–	
J Poots, Lurgan	4	9600	–	
J Ramsey, Broughshane	1	2027	–	
W A Simpson, Omagh	5	8500	–	
1 January 1936				
J Gaston, Belfast	20	29484	–	
S Girvan, Ballyclare	10	6400	–	
F Johnston, Lisburn	1	250	–	
McAllister & Co, Carrickfergus	2	950	–	
D McLarnon, Belfast	1	2634	–	
A & J Mallagh, Belfast	1	1998	–	
Jacob O'Neill, Bangor	8	13200	–	
R Owens, Belfast	3	2200	–	
J Patterson, Ballykinlar, Co Down	1	1860	–	
S Pentland, Belfast	6	5482	–	
A W Pithers, Newcastle	1	1400	–	
C Robinson, Larne	2	581	–	
M J Sawey, Newcastle	3	5900	–	
W Sloan, Belfast	5	4192	–	
W Stewart, Belfast	8	12700	–	
Stewart Bros, Portrush	4	4681	–	
16 June 1936				
W Clarke, Enniskillen	4	5050	–	
30 December 1937				
H Clements, Belfast	3	5200	–	
H Appleby, Enniskillen	2	1900	–	

The following parcel delivery services were also taken over on 1 November 1935

McFaul Bros, Larne	2332
Major J McGown (Q D), Coleraine	3070
W Magee & Sons, Belfast	6560

Eleven of the proprietors taken over in 1935/36 did not receive payment until the financial year ending 30 September 1939.

Appendix C

PUBLIC SERVICE VEHICLE OPERATORS IN ULSTER

Key

The name of each proprietor is given under the title by which his service was known to the public. In the event of a change in name, individual entries are given for each name, namely F Howe of Ballymena changed the title of his service from Dunloy Motor Service to Maine Auto Service, each of which appears in the appropriate place in the table. Information in the latter is tabulated in seven columns.

Col 1 Name under which service was known to the public

Col 2 Proprietor

Col 3 Location of office/residence of proprietor

Col 4 Date when service commenced, this may be several years before the proprietor employed mechanically propelled vehicles.

Col 5 Terminals of a busy route

Col 6 Name of new proprietor if service changed ownership

Col 7 Date of change of ownership, or closure

Many proprietors called their services by names other than their own, thus M Cassidy ran the Erne Bus Service. Furthermore, many of them added suffixes to indicate the type of service they offered, BS Bus service, MS Motor service, OS Omnibus service, TC Touring Company. Others described themselves as companies C and nearly all the remainder used no such descriptions. A few used abbreviations such as AS, MMS, MTC to indicate they considered themselves to be Auto Services, Mail Motor Services or Motor Transport Companies, these suffices are the only ones included in Column. 1.

THE REASON WHY

The Public should

SUPPORT the ULSTER PRIVATE OWNER.

We were the first to reduce Fares.
We are not asking for an Advance.
We are being Driven Off the Road by
What we consider Unfair Legislation
In favour of the 'Bus Monoply.

SUPPORT THE ULSTER PRIVATE OWNER AND FAIR PLAY.

Public Service Vehicle Operators in Ulster

1	2	3	4	5	6	7
Abernethy	H Abernethy & Sons	Ballyclare	1922	Belfast-Ballyclare	NCC	1929
Agnew	R Agnew	Portglenone	1922	Ballymena-Portglenone	NCC	1930
Agnew	W A Agnew	Belfast	1931	Larne Town Service	NIRTB	1935
Aldergrove	D Wilson	Aldergrove	1926	Belfast-Aldergrove	NIRTB	1935
Alexander	J Alexander	Lisburn	1926	Ballymena-Carnlough	BOC	1928
Anchor	P Doherty	Portstewart	1924	Coleraine-Portstewart	NCC	1929
Anderson	Mrs M Anderson	Ballynahinch	1927	B'hinch-Drumaness	Sharvin	1929
Antrim Coast	H McNeill Ltd	Larne	1898	Larne-Cushendall	NCC	1930
Ards MTC	Ards MTC Ltd	Belfast	1916	Belfast-Newtownards	BOC	1927
Ballinderry Queen	G Gale	Crumlin	1927	Belfast-Crumlin	BOC	1928
Ballycarry	R Welsh	–	1926	Belfast-Ballycarry	BOC	1928
Ballykinlar	W Huddleston	Ballydugan	1929	Downpatrick-Ballykinlar	NIRTB	1935
Ballymena-Carnlough MMS	Mrs L A Barr	Ballymena	1916	Ballymena-Carnlough	closed	1926
Ballynahinch MS	J Harrison	Ballynahinch	1923	Belfast-Ballynahinch	closed	1927
Balmoral	C McAfee	Belfast	1925	Belfast-Lurgan	BOC	1927
Bangor MS	M Morrow	Bangor	1885	Belfast-Bangor	BOC	1927
Bangor Queen	McKinstry-McCready	Bangor	1925	Belfast-Bangor	closed	1927
Bann	Bann MS Co Ltd	Kilrea	1926	Ballymena-Garvagh	Catherwood	1929
Bann	Bann MS Co Ltd	Kilrea	1926	Coleraine-Magherafelt	NCC	1929
Barkley	R Barkley	Larne	1928	Larne-Magheramourne	NIRTB	1935
Barklie & Morgan	Barklie & Morgan	Belfast	1928	Belfast City	BCT	1928
Barr	E Barr	Buncrana	1926	Derry-Buncrana	LLSR	1930
Beggs	H Beggs	Donaghadee	1926	Donaghadee-B'walter	–	–
BCDR	BCDR	Belfast	1916	Belfast-Holywood	NIRTB	1935
Belfast & District CC	Belfast & District	Belfast	1912	Tour Operator	–	–
BNCR	BNCR	Belfast	1902	Greenisland-Whiteabbey	NCC	1903
BCT	Belfast Corporation	Belfast	1926	Belfast City	City Bus	1967
BOC	BOC	Belfast	1927	Belfast-Lisburn	NIRTB	1935
Belsize	–	–	1927	Belfast-Aghalee	–	–
Bennett	J Bennett	Donaghadee	1929	Bangor-Donaghadee*	closed	1929
Blue Bird	D McLaughlin	Carndonagh	1928	Derry-Carndonagh	LLSR	1930
Blytheswood AS	J Winter	Belfast	1926	Belfast-Fivemiletown	Eclipse	1927
Borden	R C Borden	Belfast	1928	Belfast City	BCT	1929
Boyd	I & T Boyd	Clones	1933	Monaghan-Clones	GNR	1938
Boyd	J Boyd	Cushendall	1926	Cushendall-Parkmore	closed	1930
Burns	S Burns	Kilmacrenan	1928	Letterkenny-Creslough	LLSR	1930
CDMS	J Winter	Derry	1931	Non-operative	LLSR	1931
CDR	CDR	Stranorlar	1930	Killybegs-Glenties	GNR	1933
Carton	Carton	Ballynahinch	1923	Belfast-Ballynahinch	–	–
Castles	T Castles	Lurgan	1927	Lurgan-Bann Foot	McLearnon	1930
Castlewellan	P Egner	Castlewellan	1927	Downpatrick-C'wellan	BOC	1929
Catherwood	HMS Catherwood	Belfast	1925	Belfast-Portrush	NIRTB	1935
Central	H Appleby	Enniskillen	1926	Sligo-Enniskillen	NIRTB	1937
Chambers	S Chambers	Lambeg	1928	Lisburn-Ballyskeag	BOC	1931
CIE	CIE	Dublin	1945	–	active	–
Citizen	H Gray	Portadown	1927	Portadown-Lurgan	Poots	1932
Clarke	M Clarke	Leitrim, Co Down	1929	Ballynahinch-C'wellan	NIRTB	1935
Clarkes Blue Buses	W Clarke	Enniskillen	1927	Enniskillen-Pettigo	NIRTB	1935
Classic (Lisburn)	W Jellie	Lisburn	1924	Belfast-Armagh	BOC	1927
Classic (Monaghan)	J Parkes	Castleblayney	1926	Dundalk-Monaghan	GNR	1929

Clegg	J Clegg	Belfast	1927	Belfast-Bangor	BCT	1928
Coastal	Coastal BS Ltd	Portrush	1966	Coleraine-B'castle	Ulsterbus	1974
Coaster	J Heyburn Smyth	Groomsport	1921	Bangor-Groomsport	Tonic	1931
Cochrane	S Cochrane	Belfast	1921	Private Hire	–	–
Connemara	Connemara	Dublin	1928	Dublin-Derry	closed	1929
Cookstown TC	G Keane	Cookstown	1925	Belfast-Cookstown	McGucken	1926
Cosy	Maxwell & McClean	Lisburn	1927	Belfast-Hillhall	closed	1928
Coyle	P Coyle	Kerrykeel	1928	Letterkenny-Portsalon	Ward	1929
Cregan	B Cregan	Newry	1927	Newry-Forkhill	McNally	1930
Criterion	McGlade	Armagh	1927	Belfast-Armagh	BOC	1928
Crooks	J Crooks	Carrickfergus	1925	Belfast-Carrickfergus	BOC	1927
Crory	D A Crory	Rathfriland	1923	Belfast-Rathfriland	BOC	1927
Cummin	Mrs S Cummin	Lurgan	1925	Belfast-Lurgan	closed	1927
Cushendall	Henry McNeill Ltd	Larne	1921	Larne-Cushendall	NCC	1930
Davidson	D J Davidson	Aughnacloy	1927	Dungannon-Monaghan	GNR	1932
Davidson	S Davidson	Comber	1925	Belfast-Comber	BOC	1932
Diamond Bus	W Dow	Crumlin	1923	Belfast-Crumlin	GNR	1930
Dickson & Ireland	Dickson & Ireland	Belfast	1923	Tour Operator	NIRTB	1935
Doherty	Jos Doherty	Moville	1928	Derry-Moville	CDMS	1931
Dougherty	R Dougherty	Ballymena	1926	Ballymena-Kilrea	–	–
Downey	C Downey	Rathfriland	1927	Newry-Rathfriland	NIRTB	1935
Downpatrick	A Moffett	Downpatrick	1923	Belfast-Downpatrick	McCurdy & Nevin	1925
Downpatrick	McCurdy & Nixon	Downpatrick	1925	Belfast-Downpatrick	BOC	1928
Dreadnought	C H Donaghy	Omagh	1927	Derry-Omagh	GNR	1931
Dromara	M O'Reilly	Dromara	1923	Ballynahinch-Dromara	BOC	1927
Drumbo Queen	J Burton	Belfast	1927	Belfast-Drumbo	closed	1932
Drumshanbo Queen	G Alexander	Cookstown	1928	Cookstown-Pomeroy	closed	1932
Duchess	T Morgan	Maze	1926	Belfast-Donacloney	BOC	1931
Dunloy	F Howe	Ballymena	1926	Ballymena-Dunloy	Maine AS	1929
Eclipse MTC	J Winter	Belfast	1927	Belfast-Omagh	GNR	1929
Enterprise	M Morrow	Bangor	1911	Belfast-Bangor	BOC	1927
Erne	M Cassidy	Enniskillen	1929	Enniskillen-Clones	UTA	1957
Erskine	S & J Erskine	Ballyclare	1926	Belfast-Ballyclare	J McNeilly	1929
Express MC	Express MC Ltd	Belfast	1914	Belfast-Bangor	closed	1926
Fairy Queen	J Galbraith	Buncrana	1930	Derry-Buncrana	closed	–
Fairway	Fairway Ltd	Dublin	1928	Dublin-Monaghan	GNR	1929
Fallows	R Fallows	Dungiven	1929	Limavady-Dungiven	closed	1934
Favourite	J McCabe	Waringstown	1928	Lurgan-Donacloney	NIRTB	1935
Felling-Stevens	Felling-Stevens	Belfast	1921	Tour Operator	–	–
Finlay	W Finlay	Castlewellan	1884	Newcastle-C'wellan	NIRTB	1935
Fleetwing	W A Simpson	Omagh	1927	Omagh-Enniskillen	NIRTB	1935
Frizzell	A Frizzell	Portstewart	1925	Portrush-Portstewart	NCC	1930
Frontier	Poots-Dunlop	Dromore	1924	Belfast-Newry	BOC	1927
GNR	GNR	Belfast	1929	Belfast-Lisburn	NIRTB	1935
GSR	GSR	Dublin	1927	Dublin-Cavan	IOC	1927
Galt	WHC Galt	Coleraine	1925	Coleraine-Garvagh	closed	1927
Garrett & Robinson	Garrett & Robinson	Belfast	1926	Belfast-Killyleagh	closed	1928
Gaston	J Gaston	Belfast	1920	Tour Operator	NIRTB	1935
Gibson	Gibson	Belfast	1926	Tour Operator	–	–
Gillespie	SH Gillespie	Holywood	1927	Belfast-Holywood	BCDR	1929

Girvan	S Girvan	Ballyclare	1921	Tour Operator	NIRTB	1935
Glider	J Poots	Dromore	1926	Lurgan-Portadown	NIRTB	1935
Gordon	Gordon (1928) Ltd	Cavan	1928	Dublin-Cavan	GNR	1931
Gregory	E Gregory	Hillsborough	1927	Lisburn-Dunmurry	BCT	1928
Grew	J Grew	Portadown	1928	Portadown Station Bus	GNR	1931
Hamilton	F Hamilton	Portaferry	1915	Newtownards-Portaferry	Ards	1927
Hard Rocks	E W McCreery	Lisbellaw	1928	Enniskillen-Tempo	Clarke	1933
Harrison	S Harrison	Edenderry	1927	Belfast-Edenderry	D Lawther	1930
Hawthorn Tours	D McLarnon	Belfast	1932	Local Markets	NIRTB	1935
Hay	W Hay	–	1927	Cullybackey-Rasharkin	R C Smyth	1928
Heather Queen	Mrs M Charlton	Omagh	1926	Omagh-Cookstown	NIRTB	1935
Heddles Islandmagee	S Heddle	Ballycarry	1920	Belfast-Islandmagee	BOC	1927
Henry's	S S Henry	Portstewart	1890	Portrush-Portstewart	NIRTB	1935
Henry-Hunter	–	–	1926	Belfast-Garvagh	–	–
Hill	W F Hill	Omagh	1929	Omagh-Baronscourt	Mrs M Charlton	1931
Hobsons	W E Hobson	Dungannon	1927	Dungannon-Cookstown	NIRTB	1935
Hutchinson	Hutchinson Bros	Limavady	1922	Derry-Coleraine	Catherwood	1928
IOC	GSR	Dublin	1927	Derry-Sligo	Catherwood	1928
Imperial (Donaghadee)	W Crawford	Donaghadee	1925	Belfast-Donaghadee	Baird & Weir	1930
Imperial (Donaghadee)	Baird & Weir	Belfast	1930	Belfast-Donaghadee	NIRTB	1935
Imperial (Portadown)	J Bleakney	Portadown	1927	Portadown-Tanderagee	United	1929
Irish Sleeper	Irish Sleeper	Dublin	1928	Dublin-Cork	closed	1929
Independent	R A Johnston	Belfast	1928	Belfast-Dungiven	NIRTB	1935
International	Baird & Weir	Belfast	1927	Belfast-Dublin	Catherwood	1929
Irish MTC	JWC Butler	Edinburgh	1907	Newtownards-Portaferry	closed	1908
Irvine	W Irvine	Larne	1926	Tour Operator	NIRTB	1935
Irvine	–	–	1926	–	closed	1927
Irwin J	J Irwin	Newry	1921	Newry-Rathfriland	F Revels	1929
Irwin	J & R Irwin	Lurgan	1926	Belfast-Lurgan	GNR	1929
Island	R Strahan	Islandmagee	1923	Ballycarry-Islandmagee	NCC	1932
Jamieson	J Jamieson	Broughshane	1927	Ballymena-Sheddings	NIRTB	1935
Johnston	E Johnston	Ballynahinch	1922	Belfast-Ballynahinch	closed	1927
Johnston	E Johnston	Ballynahinch	1927	Comber-Killyleagh	closed	–
Johnston	F Johnston	Larne	–	Tour Operator	NIRTB	1935
Kane	J Kane	Culdaff	1929	Derry-Culdaff	LLSR	1930
Kearney	D Kearney	Malin	1927	Derry-Malin	CDMS	1931
Keenan	Keenan Bros	Carlingford	1929	Newry-Carlingford	closed	1929
Kelly	P Kelly	Kerrykeel	1928	Letterkenny-Kerrykeel	Ward	1929
Kelvin	–	Cavan	1928	Cavan-Dublin	GNR	1931
Kennedy	Mrs R Kennedy	Portrush	1924	Coleraine-Portrush	NCC	1929
Kerr	W Kerr	Toomebridge	1928	Ballymena-Toomebridge	NIRTB	1935
Knutt Charabanc	Tinsley	Belfast	1924	Tour Operator	–	–
LLSR	LLSR	Derry	1929	Derry-Buncrana	active	–
Lagan Queen	J McLearnon	Lurgan	1928	Lurgan-Aghagallon	NIRTB	1935
Lancia	Eadie & Tornie	Newtownards	1925	Belfast-Newtownards	Moss	1926
Largy Bus	W Wilson	Crumlin	1926	Armagh-Fivemiletown	J Winter	1927

Larnes Pride	R Patterson	Belfast	1925	Belfast-Larne	closed	1927
Lawther	Lawther D	Dunmurry	1925	Belfast-Drumbo	NIRTB	1935
Lawther	Lawther J&R	Ballywalter	1928	Newtownards-B'walter	NIRTB	1935
Lindsay	Lindsay J	Saintfield	1926	Belfast-Saintfield	closed	–
Lisnagarvey Queen	G Gillespie	Lisburn	1926	Belfast-Ravernet	BOC	1927
Londonderry City	L'derry Corporation	Derry	1919	City Bus Service	Catherwood	1929
Lord Leitrim	Lord Leitrim	Rosapenna	1903	Strabane-Rosapenna	closed	–
Lough Neagh Queen	H Flack	Coagh	1925	Belfast-Cookstown	NCC	1929
Lough Swilly BS	P Doherty	London	1981	North West Donegal	Active	–
Lyttle	D Lyttle	Castlerock	1927	Coleraine-Castlerock	–	–
Magee	W Magee & Son	Belfast	–	Parcel delivery service	NIRTB	1935
Magnet	A W Gordon	Cavan	1925	Dublin-Cavan	Gordon (1928) Ltd	1928
Maid of Mourne	T Wallace	Killyleagh	1921	Comber-Killyleagh	S G McFarlane	1925
Maine AS	F Howe	Ballymena	1929	Ballymena-Dunloy	NIRTB	1935
Major	W J Clements	Belfast	1925	City Bus Service	BCT	1947
Mallagh	H & K Mallagh	Belfast	–	Tour Operator	NIRTB	1935
Marlowe	Miss M Marlowe	Omagh	1929	Omagh-Baronscourt	M Charleton	1931
Martin	Mrs E G Martin	Belfast	1925	Belfast-Ballynahinch	BOC	1927
Martin	H R Martin	Belfast	1927	Belfast-Carrickfergus	NCC	1929
Martin	W Martin	Lisburn	1928	Belfast-Purdysburn	Nevin	1932
Martin	W E Martin	Rathfriland	1926	Rathfriland-Ballyroney	NIRTB	1935
Mawhinney	J Mawhinney	Belfast	1925	Belfast-Parkgate	R Dow`	1932
Merrilees	S B Merrilees	Enniskillen	1927	Enniskillen -Derrygonnelly	W Clarke	1927
Mewhirter	JC Mewhirter	Belfast	1933	Belfast-Parkgate	NCC	1934
Millisle Queen	Kane Bros	Millisle	1926	Belfast-Millisle	NIRTB	1935
Moneyreagh	R Gilliland	Moneyreagh	1921	Belfast-Ballygowan	–	1935
Montgomery	T Montgomery	Buckna	1927	Ballymena-Buckna	NIRTB	1935
Moore	Moore Bros	Donaghadee	1922	Tour Operator	–	–
Morris	J Morris	Downpatrick	1927	Belfast-Downpatrick**	closed	1928
Moss Line	A J Moss	Newtownards	1920	Newtownards-P'ferry	BOC	1927
Mourne	D A McAtee	Kilkeel	1924	Belfast-Kilkeel	BOC	1933
Mourne Mountain TC	G B Morgan	Warrenpoint	1913	Tour Operator	–	–
Murphy	P Murphy	Ballymena	–	Tour Operator	NIRTB	1935
McAllister	J McAllister	Larne	1926	Larne-Cushendun	NIRTB	1935
McCann	W J McCann	Richhill	1927	Armagh-Richhill	–	1927
McClements	T McClements	Belfast	1924	Belfast-Holywood	closed	1929
McCourt	J McCourt	Newry	1926	Newry-Crossmaglen	BOC	1928
McDonald	McDonald	Holywood	1929	Belfast-Holywood	closed	–
McDonald	J McDonald	Coleraine	1926	Coleraine-Ballycastle	NCC	1929
McDowell	McDowell	Omagh	1927	Omagh-Dungannon	Eclipse	1928
McFarland	F&N McFarland	Crossgar	1925	Belfast-Derryboy	BOC	1928
McFarlane	S G McFarlane	Belfast	1925	Belfast-Killyleagh	BOC	1927
McFaul	McFaul Bros	Larne	–	Parcel Delivery Service	NIRTB	1935
McGirr	J McGirr	Dungannon	1930	Dungannon-Omagh	Hobson	1930
McGivern	R McGivern	Carrowdore	1919	N'ards-Carrowdore	NIRTB	1935
McGucken	J McGucken	Cookstown	1925	Belfast-Cookstown	BOC	1927
McKees	McKees MS Co Ltd	Belfast	1924	Belfast-Whitehead	BOC	1927
McKee	T McKee	Lisburn	1928	Belfast-Ballyskeagh	Chambers	1930
McLaughlin	D McLaughlin	Carndonagh	1928	Derry-Carndonagh	LLSR	1930

McMillan	–	–	1926	Belfast-Parkgate	–	–
McNally	M McNally	Newry	1927	Newry-Dromintee	NIRTB	1935
McNeilly	J McNeilly	Belfast	1924	Belfast-Randalstown	BOC	1927
NCC	NCC	Belfast	1903	Greenisland-Whiteabbey	LMS	1923
NIRTB	NIRTB	Belfast	1935	Belfast-Lisburn	UTA	1948
Nelson	F H Nelson	Ballybay	1929	Armagh-Ballybay	BCT	1928
Nesbitt	J Nesbitt	Warrenpoint	1928	Newry-Milltown	BOC	1930
Nevin	W Nevin	Belfast	1932	Belfast-Drumbo	NIRTB	1935
North Star	A Moore	Ballymena	1927	Belfast-Ballycastle	Catherwood	1928
North of Ireland OC	NIOC	Belfast	1926	Holding Company	BOC	1927
Norton	Norton & Co	Kilkeel	1916***	Warrenpoint-Kilkeel	GNR	1930
Nugent	T Nugent	Keady	1926	Armagh-Keady	GNR	1931
Nutt's Saloon	RJP Nutt	Limavady	1922	Derry-Coleraine	Catherwood	1929
Nutt	WF Nutt	Belfast	1929	Belfast-Drumbo	Burton	1930
O'Brien	J O'Brien	Portavogie	1911	Newtownards-Portavogie	Ards	1916
Omeath	P Maguire	Omeath	1928	Newry-Omeath	GNR	1932
O'Reilly MMS	M O'Reilly	Dromara	1923	Ballynahinch-Dromara	BOC	1927
Owens	R Owens	Belfast	–	Tour Operator	NIRTB	1935
Paragon	Bell & Paisley	Belfast	1925	Belfast-Magherafelt	BOC	1928
Parkes	J Parkes	Lurgan	1921	Tour Operator	–	–
Pentland	S Pentland	Belfast	1921	Tour Operator	NIRTB	1935
Petticrew	D Petticrew	Belfast	1927	Tour Operator	BCT	1928
Phair	Phair Bros	Belturbet	1928	Enniskillen-Cavan	GNR	1932
Phantom	Edgar Bros	Belfast	1926	Belfast-Kilkeel	BOC	1928
Picken	S Picken	Belfast	1925	Belfast-Cookstown	–	–
Pickie Tours	J McCartney	Newtownards	1924	Tour Operator	NIRTB	1935
Pilot (The)	Six Counties MC Ltd	Portadown	1924	Portadown-Banbridge	BOC	1927
Pioneer	Jacob O'Neill	Bangor	1913	Belfast-Bangor	NIRTB	1935
Pioneer	J McCartney	Newtownards	1924	Belfast-Newtownards	NIRTB	1935
Pithers	A W Pithers	Newcastle	–	Tour Operator	NIRTB	1936
Portaferry Mail	Ferguson & Graham	Belfast	1908	Belfast-Portaferry	Hamilton	1915
Princess	Weatherup, Smith & McNeilly	Belfast	1924	Belfast-Ballymena	BOC	1927
Purdysburn	McCreight & Ross	Belfast	1927	Belfast-Purdysburn	J McNeilly	1930
Purdysburn	J McNeilly	Belfast	1930	Belfast-Purdysburn	NIRTB	1935
Quayle	HF Quayle	Strangford	1919	Downpatrick-S'ford	closed	1921
QD	Major J McGown	Coleraine	–	Parcel Delivery Service	NIRTB	1935
Radford	Radford	Warrenpoint	1913	Warrenpoint-Rostrevor	–	–
Ramsey	J Ramsey	Broughshane	1928	Ballymena-Broughshane	NIRTB	1935
Ramsey	W Ramsey	Lisburn	1925	Tour Operator	closed	–
Regent	W Davidson	Coalisland	1929	Dungannon-Coalisland	Hobson	1931
Regent	WH Reay	Belfast	1928	Dungannon-Cookstown	Hobson	1929
Reliable AS	NW Brodie	Coalisland	1925	Dungannon-Cookstown	Regent	1928
Reliance	A Stringer	Belfast	1908	Newtownards-Portaferry	Hamilton	1915
Reliance (The)	J & RJ Steen	Newtown-hamilton	1920	Newry-Newtownhamilton	NIRTB	1935
Renown	S Alexander	Markethill	1926	Belfast-Newry	Lewis & Smith	1927
Renown	Lewis & Smith	Lambeg	1927	Belfast-Markethill	GNR	1930
Repulse	McAlinden & McSherry	Lurgan	1928	Lurgan-Aghalee	GNR	1930

Revels	R Revels	Rathfriland	1929	Newry-Rathfriland	Stevenson	1930
Roberts	Roberts Bros	Derry	1912	Derry-Moville	CDMS	1931
Robinson	C Robinson	Larne	–	Tour Operator	NIRTB	1935
Rosevale	Buchanan & Cunningham	–	1927	Belfast-Broomhedge	BOC	1927
Russell	Russell, H	Holywood	1926	Belfast-Holywood	BCDR	1929
SOS	Mrs A Sloan	Kilkeel	1928	Newry-Kilkeel	BOC	1932
Sanspareil	S Sands	Belfast	1925	Belfast-Crumlin	–	–
Sawey	M Sawey	Newcastle	–	Tour Operator	NIRTB	1936
Scott	W Scott	Belfast	1927	Belfast-Purdysburn	closed	1930
Shaftesbury Charabanc	–	Belfast	1928	Tour Operator	–	–
Shank	J Shank	Belfast	1925	Tour Operator	–	–
Sharvin RMMS	Sharvin Bros	Strangford	1920	Downpatrick-Strangford	BOC	1933
Shilliday	J Shilliday	Bangor	1913	Bangor-Donaghadee	Moore Bros	1926
Skelton	Skelton	Belfast	1925	Belfast-Ballycarry	–	–
Sloan	W Sloan	Belfast	–	Tour Operator	NIRTB	1935
Smyth	R C Smyth	–	1929	Cullybackey-Rasharkin	–	–
Spence	E & F Spence	Hillsborough	1928	Belfast-Dromara	BOC	1930
Spence	Spence & McCrea	Dromore	1923	Belfast-Dromore	BOC	1927
Stevenson	R Stevenson & Son	Rathfriland	1919	Rathfriland-C'wellan	NIRTB	1935
Stewart	Stewart Bros	Garvagh	1915	Coleraine-Maghera	NCC	1929
Stewart	Mrs WA Stewart	Donaghadee	1926	Bangor-Donaghadee	Imperial BS	1929
Strangford	Conway Bros	Strangford	1923	Downpatrick-S'ford	Sharvin	1929
Suffolk	Baird & Weir	Belfast	1929	Belfast-Lisburn	R Dow	1930
Sureline Coaches	Sureline Coaches Ltd	Lurgan	1966	Lurgan-Banbridge	closed	1987
Swift Services	WF Nutt	Belfast	1926	Belfast-Holywood	closed	1928
Swilly Queen	John Doherty	Buncrana	1926	Derry-Buncrana	LLSR	1930
Tonic	JH O'Neill	Bangor	1927	Bangor District	NIRTB	1935
Triumph	T Spence	Belfast	1927	Belfast-Ballynahinch	NIRTB	1930
Ulster & General MTC	UGMTC	Belfast	1914	Comber-Killyleagh	McFarlane	1921
Ulster General OC	UGOC	London	1927	Non-operating	closed	1927
Ulster Passenger Bus Combine	T Clements	Belfast	1930	Non-operating	closed	1930
United	Ulster Motor Service Co Ltd	Tandragee	1927	Newry-Portadown	GNR	1929
Viking	J Coey	Bangor	1928	Bangor-Donaghadee	BOC	1929
Violet	Crothers & Dugan	Lisburn	1924	Belfast-Dromara	BOC	1927
Wallace	A Wallace	Lurgan	1928	Lurgan-Portadown	T Castles	1929
Wallace	T Wallace	Killyleagh	1919	Comber-Killyleagh	G McFarlane	1925
Ward	Ward Bros	Kerrykeel	1927	Derry-Letterkenny	CDMS	1931
Warke	JB Warke	Castlerock	1926	Coleraine-Castlerock	–	–
Wee McGregor	Scott & McGregor	Hillsborough	1927	Belfast-Dromara	BOC	1927
Weir	D Weir	Bushmills	1927	Coleraine-Bushmills	Catherwood	1929
Weir	TV Weir	Newtownards	1933	Belfast-Newtownards	NIRTB	1935
Wellington	A Moore	Ballymena	1926	Belfast-Ballymena	J McNeilly	1929
White	JD White	Bushmills	1927	Coleraine-Bushmills	Catherwood	1929
White	WE White	Enniskillen	1928	Enniskillen-Carrick on Shannon	closed	1929

White Star Line	W Stewart	Belfast	1928	Tour Operator	NIRTB	1935
Whiteheather	–	Belfast	1921	Tour Operator	–	–
Williamson	Williamson	Portadown	1927	Armagh-Ballybay	closed	1927
Wilson	J Wilson	Belfast	1927	Belfast-Purdysburn	NIRTB	1935
Windsor	W Patterson	Belfast	1926	Belfast-Aghalee	R Patterson	1929
Windsor	R Patterson	Belfast	1928	Belfast-Stoneyford	NIRTB	1935
Woodburn	R Dow	Belfast	1930	Belfast-Lisburn	NIRTB	1935
Wright	–	Portadown	1925	Belfast-Ballymena	–	–
W W Charabancs	–	Belfast	1927	–	–	–
Yellow Line	H McAnulty	Warrenpoint	1915****	Warrenpoint-Kilkeel	NIRTB	1935

* Probably never was operational
** Via Crossgar and Killyleagh
*** Date when Norton & Co acquired their first bus.
**** Date when McAnulty acquired his first bus.

Time Table from 1st July to 30th September.

CHAR-A-BANC SERVICE

BETWEEN

Portstewart Old Golf House & New Golf Links.

	a.m.	a.m.	a.m.	p.m.	p.m.	p.m.	p.m.	p.m.	p.m.	p.m.
Portstewart Old Club House—Dep.	9-40	10- 0	10-20	12-30a	12-50	2-30	2-50	4-40	5-30	6-30
Portstewart New Golf Links—arr.	9-50	10-10	10-30	12-40	1- 0	2-40	3- 0	4-50	5-40	6-40

a WILL START FROM POST OFFICE.

	a.m.	a.m.	a.m.	p.m.	p.m.	p.m.	p.m.	p.m.	p.m.	p.m.
Portstewart New Golf Links—Dep.	9-50	10-10	10-30	12-40	1- 0	2-40	3- 0	4-50	5-40	6-40
Portstewart Old Club House—arr.	10- 0	10-20	10-40	12-50	1-10	2-50	3-10	5- 0	5-50	6-50

FARES: 3d, Single.

Golfers must have preference of Seating Accommodation.

"Northern Constitution," Coleraine.

Index

GENERAL INDEX

PERSONAL NAMES INDEX